THE YACHTSMAN'S GUIDE TO
calculator
navigation
by Stafford Campbell

YACHTING/BOATING BOOKS·ZIFF-DAVIS PUBLISHING
COMPANY   NEW YORK

Contents

Foreword

The elements of coastwise and celestial navigation have been described in my two preceding books in the Yachtsman's Guide series, *The Yachtsman's Guide to Coastwise Navigation* and *The Yachtsman's Guide to Celestial Navigation.* The present text is intended to translate those fundamentals into mathematical form, and to explain how to perform the solutions rapidly and simply on a modern, hand-held, electronic calculator.

The list of programs includes the principal exercises encountered by the small-boat navigator under way, as well as some additional ones useful in deriving auxiliary and planning information. The programs themselves have been designed primarily with the yachtsman in mind, and were selected, developed, and tested in the course of a transpacific voyage aboard the containership

S.S. *President Eisenhower.* The cooperation and encouragement of the ship's officers is gratefully acknowledged.

While the program selection, design, and subsequent testing is as thorough as I know how to make it, the material in this text is presented without representation or warranty of any kind, and the author and publisher assume no responsibility or liability, consequential or otherwise, arising from its use.

S.C.
May, 1979

Introduction

The rapidity with which the hand-held, or "personal," calculator has evolved is one of the technical phenomena of our times. The quiet revolution has had its impact on all of us, perhaps even greater than we realize, in substituting almost instantaneous, accurate computation for the error-prone tedium of traditional mathematical methods. In fact, those who make no pretense of their mathematical abilities can now solve problems that were customarily within the province of the highly trained specialist.

The hand-held calculator is an outgrowth of the progress in solid-state electronic technology—that which saw the vacuum tube and hand-wired circuitry replaced with miniaturized transistors and printed circuits. Today, for example, you can carry more computing power in your pocket than was available in the largest instruments before the 1950s, and at a price about one ten-thousandth as much. There is little wonder that people in all walks of life, and navigators among them, are using hand-held calculators to ease the tasks of their trades.

For the navigator, the major advantage to be gained from a calculator is the reduction in both the time required and the possibilities for error inherent in tedious manual computations, freeing the operator to undertake a greater number of exercises and thereby improving his technical capability.

The object of this text is to introduce the small-boat navigator to hand-held calculators, to help him select one suited to his needs, to discuss the operating aspects, and to present sample programs—designed for a minimum practical calculator—to solve most of the common navigational exercises. While these programs constitute a basic library, after you have become familiar with the techniques involved it should be possible for you to add more programs of your own, or to reorganize those presented here, in order to best serve your personal requirements.

It is not practicable to deal with the individual operating details of every model or manufacture of calculator. The instruction book or owner's manual is the proper source for that. It follows, too, that the advantage of the calculator over manual or tabular methods can be maximized only when the operator has gained familiarity and facility with his particular instrument. "Know your calculator" may seem elementary, but it is not-to-be-overlooked advice.

It should be recognized at the outset that a calculator, just like the old-fashioned adding machine, doesn't alter the mathematical principles in a problem but simply facilitates its numerical computation. The practical navigator, consequently, will be well grounded in the principles of the art, and will benefit from his calculator in the convenience and speed of the computation, but not as a substitute for knowledge. Remember, too, that a delicate electronic instrument in the environment of a small boat at sea is not immune to failure, and the navigator who is totally reliant on his calculator may one day be in for an unpleasant surprise.

Consistent with these thoughts, this book presupposes that you understand the fundamentals of the common evolutions in navigation—not necessarily every mathematical formula and detail, but at least the underlying principles. Should you be rusty in this area, you can refer to the earlier texts in this series, mentioned in the Foreword, or to one of the classic navigation references—Bowditch, *American Practical Navigator* (Defense Mapping Agency Hydrographic/Topographic Center, Washington) or Dutton, *Dutton's Navigation and Piloting* (Naval Institute Press, Annapolis).

On the other hand, a graduate degree in mathematics is not at all necessary either. Many of us will have had an introduction to geometry and to the natural trigonometric functions at the secondary school level, and that is about as complex as most navigation problems become. Most problems are solved simply by applying the basic principles step by step, letting the calculator perform the tedious operations.

This is not, therefore, primarily a mathematical text. The range of navigation problems has been organized according to the nature of the mathematical operation involved, and arranged in an ascending order of complexity. In the more advanced solutions, the formulae and method of approach have been noted where it might contribute to better understanding, but for practical purposes the programs can be utilized just by following the steps as outlined. It is recommended to the new arrival on the calculator scene that the programs be reviewed in the order presented the first time through. After familiarization, the individual sequences can be consulted directly as a reference whenever the need arises.

Let's start at the beginning and consider what kind of an instrument you will want for your practice of calculator navigation.

1. Selecting a Calculator

The first problem facing the navigator who wants to take advantage of modern calculator technology is the very basic one of selecting an instrument most practicable for his needs. Since the multiplicity of models currently available encompasses such a wide spectrum of performance—not to mention price—some organized thinking is in order before rushing out to make the purchase. The best way to go about this preparatory step is to identify the types of problems *you* expect to solve with *your* calculator, and then review the equipment that can handle them. In other words, what combination of functions or features should your calculator possess?

To guide you toward the answer, Figure 1-1 classifies the mathematical level of the various types of navigation problems, with examples of each, and, in the third column, lists the incremental calculator functions used in the

Desirable Functions in a Hand-held Calculator For Navigation

Level of Navigation Problem	*Example of Type*	*Incremental Calculator Functions Desired*
Arithmetic	Time-Speed-Distance Horizon Distance Sextant Corrections	Four arithmetic functions $\div$ $\times$ $-$ $+$ Square roots $\sqrt{x}$ Sexagesimal/Decimal conversions DMS.DD Change Sign key $+/-$
Vector Arithmetic	Current Sailing (Course and Speed Made Good)	Register Exchange key $x \rightleftarrows y$ Rectangular/Polar coordinate conversion $P{\rightarrow}R$ Two addressable memories, STO, capable of register arithmetic
Plane Trigonometry	Current Sailing (Course to Steer)	Natural trigonometric functions and inverse functions $\sin$ $\cos$ $\tan$ Total of five memories
	Vertical Angles	Squares; One level of parentheses x^2 $($ $)$
	Height of Tide	Second level of parentheses
Spherical Trigonometry	Sight Reduction	Third addressable memory

Figure 1-1.

solution. Each function listed, you will notice, is *in addition to* those preceding, one or more of which may also be required in the computation. To solve a problem involving sextant corrections, for example, you would want the sexagesimal/decimal conversion feature in addition to the arithmetic functions required for the first level of computations. One point should be clarified, however; the listings in the table are not absolute. That is to say it may be entirely possible to solve certain problems without the benefit of all the listed functions, although doing so may be much more cumbersome. On the other hand, some solutions may be made still easier or quicker with more calculator features. The objective of the table, therefore, is to suggest the minimum *practical* functions to solve the problem with a minimum number of keystrokes. Where the keypunch sequence is performed automatically, as in the more sophisticated programmable calculators, the number of steps may not be as important, but in the manual models, on which almost everyone learns, features that contribute to the shortest solution will be those you will want.

A fact to remember in the selection process is that most calculators—except, perhaps, for those prewired expressly for navigation—are designed for a wide range of problem solving of which navigation is only one small part. As a consequence, a general-purpose calculator with features to handle the more complex navigation exercises will generally have the capability to solve a vast number of nonnavigational problems, and will very likely offer some functions that will never be used in navigation.

Adding somewhat further to the possibility of confusion is the terminology, which, in the rapidly developing market for small calculators, has not yet seen complete standardization. Happily, however, common nomenclature is starting to become evident among the major suppliers, and it is increasingly practicable to relate one manufacturer's product to another's. The best advice, in any case, is to identify your range of problems in the navigational hierarchy, noting the features or functions needed to accommodate them, and to start with the simplest model calculator embodying those minimum functions, moving up to the more sophisticated equipment as you progress.

Calculators are offered in several different categories with which you should be familiar before your shopping expedition starts. Should you plan to confine your use to arithmetical applications, a simple four-function (add, subtract, multiply, and divide) model, some of which are available for under $10, is really all you need. As you increase the complexity of the navigation problems you want to solve, you will advance to the next plateau—the "slide rule" or scientific types that add the capability to perform trigonometric and other higher functions. Manual, "slide rule" models, so called because they are rapidly replacing that venerable device, can be had for under $50, and quite fine ones for under $100. Many of this type have additional capabilities, such as multiple memories, which can store intermediate data in a long calculation, saving a number of duplicate keystrokes and considerable time in the process.

In essence, the solution of *any* calculator problem consists of a sequence of keypunches. The fewer of these the operator has to perform, the shorter the time required, and, usually, the smaller the chance for error. Accordingly, as the complexity of the problems and the corresponding number of keystrokes increased (often into the hundreds), calculator manufacturers met the challenge with an advanced level of instruments they called "preprogrammed" and "programmable" calculators. These adhere to exactly the same mathematical principles as their less sophisticated kin, but their capabilities save the operator many keystrokes.

The "preprogrammed" group is capable of performing certain sequences with the depression of a single key. Most scientific calculators have at least some preprogrammed functions, such as square roots or the value of π, while other, special-purpose models, may be "hard-wired" to perform complex sequences such as great-circle computations or other navigational specialties. These special-purpose instruments, which are themselves in a period of rapid development, may be of particular interest to the navigator who uses his calculator exclusively for the solution of a preselected set of navigation problems. Specialized navigation calculators are discussed in more detail later in this chapter.

Among the general-purpose calculators, the programmable group is the ultimate in sophistication and versatility. Their outstanding feature is the ability to accept an entire keystroke sequence for storage in a program memory before the solution begins. The operator has only to enter the initial data and start the program, which will then step through the prearranged keystroke routine internally. This is a particularly attractive feature for the navigator who must solve multiple-step problems repetitiously, and it explains why this kind of instrument is seen more and more frequently in the navigation departments of merchant ships.

The programmable category is further subdivided into two types. The first acquires its program by punching the keystroke sequence into a program memory, and the memory is engaged, after the variable data is entered, to complete the computation. Only one program at a time can be handled by these "keyboard programmable" instruments, and it is lost when another program replaces it or, with the exception of a few recent models that will retain a sequence for some time, when the calculator is turned off. Some of the better keyboard programmables sell today for under $200, and the range of problems they can handle extends well beyond the needs of the practicing navigator.

The most advanced of the programmable calculators is the type that can store keystroke sequences on magnetic tapes or modular chips. They are referred to as "fully programmable," or, more properly, as card- or chip-programmed. On some models the operator can even create his own programs to be stored permanently on the magnetic strips. In operation, the program is selected, fed into the calculator's program memory, and the variable input data introduced. The calculator then steps through the preset sequence automatically, displaying within a few seconds the numerical solution. These fully programmable calculators have the potential of offering the most significant reduction in computation time, as well as in error possibility, and, where the economics are justifiable, are often the choice of professional navigators.

To give you an idea of the economics involved, as well as the rapidity of change in the field, the Hewlett-Packard Model HP–65 fully programmable calculator cost about $800 in the mid-1970s. It accommodates programs up to one hundred steps long on magnetic strips. Fantastic? Consider that less than three years later, Hewlett-Packard's HP–67 offered the ability to store more than twice the program-steps at less than half the cost. And Texas Instruments, another leader in the field, offers a still greater program-step capability, if that is your key criterion, at a competitive price. You can be sure that still further advances are on the way.

Naturally, all the elementary grade problems can be handled with great ease on the advanced, general-purpose instruments, so it really comes down to a question of paying your money and taking your choice of arithmetic or scientific, manual or programmable, single or fully programmable—all depending on the classes of problems you expect to solve and how much the convenience of making fewer keypunches manually is worth to you.

You may be quite decided as to what level of capability you want in your hand-held calculator, but you have still one more choice to make—the choice between the two competing logics, or "languages," that modern calculators employ. The two are called "algebraic logic" (or "entry"), and "Reverse Polish Notation" (RPN). The difference in operation between these two forms of address is discussed in Chapter 2. Hewlett-Packard, probably the first company to achieve widespread distribution of scientific calculators, employs RPN, while most of the other manufacturers today espouse algebraic logic. In my opinion, for the types of problems normally encountered by the practicing navigator, the logic employed by a particular calculator is less important than its list of functions. As a result, the deciding factor in selecting the form of logic is primarily subjective—which form of address you can work with most readily. Even more important is the choice of a well-made instrument capable of withstanding the rigors of shipboard life. An inoperative calculator, regardless of its features, is less than useless.

The "hard-wired" navigational calculators represent a special class, and one that is evolving rapidly in itself. The principal entries in the field today are the Tamaya NC-2 and NC-77 models and the Plath Navicomp. The NC-2 was the first widely sold specialized navigation instrument on the American market. It comes prewired for the quick and automatic solution of some nine programs preselected by the manufacturer. In addition, many navigation problems that cannot be solved by one of the built-in programs can be computed manually in the "normal calculator mode." A noteworthy feature of this instrument is its dialogue system, which calls for entries in the proper order by means of symbols in the display and similarly identifies the answers. The NC-2 system has definite advantages over general-purpose instruments when the navigator is inexperienced or if he is not dealing with navigational problems on a calculator regularly.

A newer version of the Tamaya calculator is the NC-77, which has retained all the desirable features of the NC-2, has increased the number of prewired programs to about twenty, and has expanded the capability for problem solving in the manual calculator mode. The preselected programs in the NC-77 are most of those the small-boat navigator would be called on to solve, and the calculator also provides built-in astronomical data for GHA of Aries and for GHA and declination of the sun. These, together with the Equation of Time, are programs otherwise reserved to the most sophisticated, fully programmable instruments.

Going a step further, Plath has introduced the Navicomp, which is primarily a celestial navigation instrument, although some other navigation exercises can be solved on its manual keyboard. The particular feature of the Plath, in addition to its preprogrammed astronomical data for most of the navigational bodies, is the use of an internal quartz chronometer that can be accessed at the moment of an observation to enter automatically the correct almanac data in the sight-reduction solution. The day may be coming when the sextant reading can be fed electronically into such a navigation calculator and the entire process from sight taking to fix automatized.

In the meantime, specialized navigation calculators are affected by one circumstance that may have influence on the navigator's purchase decision. Existing in a specialized and limited market, such instruments' prices can hardly be expected to be competitive with the mass-marketed, general-purpose calculators, and this is usually the case. On the other hand, the hard-wired instruments may often speed up your computations and, through the reduction in keypunching, reduce the chance for error.

Have we seen the ultimate level of development in the hand-held calculator? Considering the rapidity of the evolution to date, I'm sure we have not, and when a further breakthrough is made in the amount of data these little marvels can absorb and display, a new generation of instruments, approaching a true pocket computer, will become available. The happy circumstance has been that with each new generation calculators have increased in capability while becoming more competitive in cost. To postpone your involvement, however, is to postpone the day you are able to enjoy the benefits offered. As a consequence, I strongly encourage interested navigators to acquire, master, and utilize the present generation of hand-held calculators as a tool for learning, for its immediate convenience, and as a leg up on the advances to come.

2. Calculator Operation

Having considered the *selection* of a hand-held calculator, let's turn our attention to the *operation,* with particular regard to the solution of navigation problems. Although no two makes or models are exactly alike, some standardization, as has been pointed out earlier, has taken place in the industry, and a number of operations are common to all instruments.

To illustrate, there are shown in Figures 2-1 through 2-4 the keyboards of four currently popular models: the Radio Shack EC-495, Texas Instruments TI-55, Hewlett-Packard HP-67, and Tamaya NC-77. You can see at a glance that the numerical portion of the keyboard, called the digit entry keys, is similar in all models, with the four arithmetic function keys arranged in a vertical column at the right, in the order $\boxed{\div}$ $\boxed{\times}$ $\boxed{-}$ $\boxed{+}$ for the calculators using algebraic logic, and in the reverse order, at the

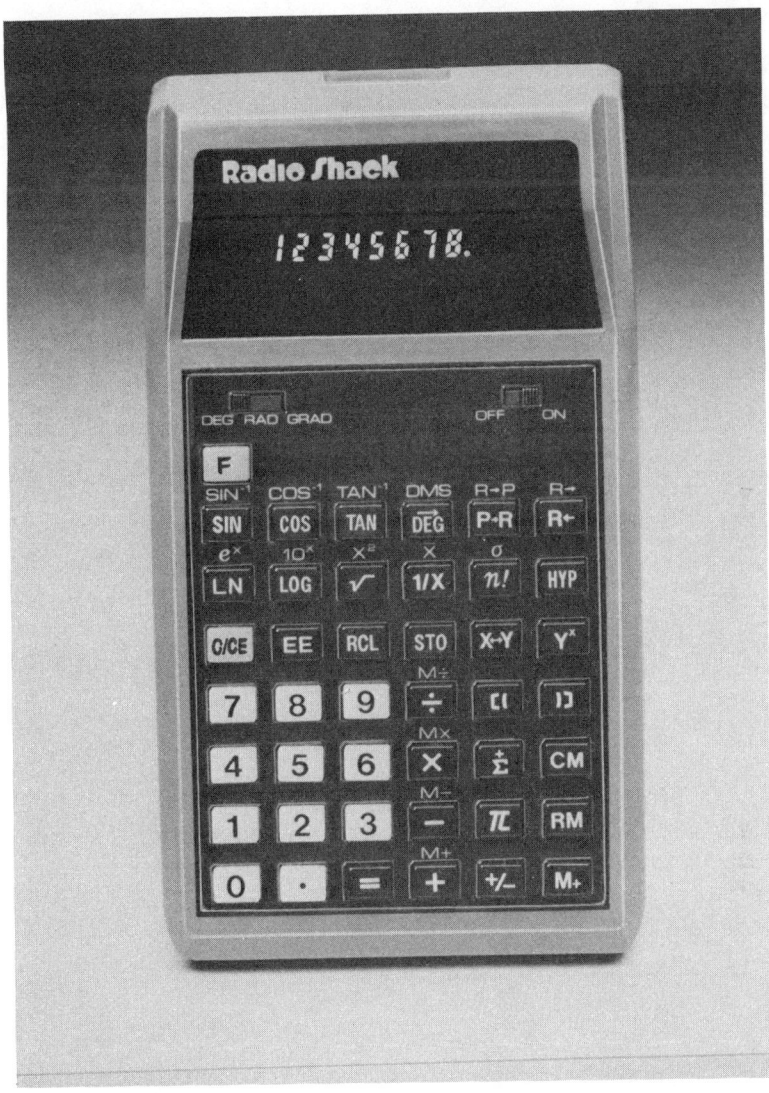

Figure 2-1. Radio Shack Model EC-495. A budget-priced, manually operated, scientific calculator having all the functions necessary to perform navigation solutions.

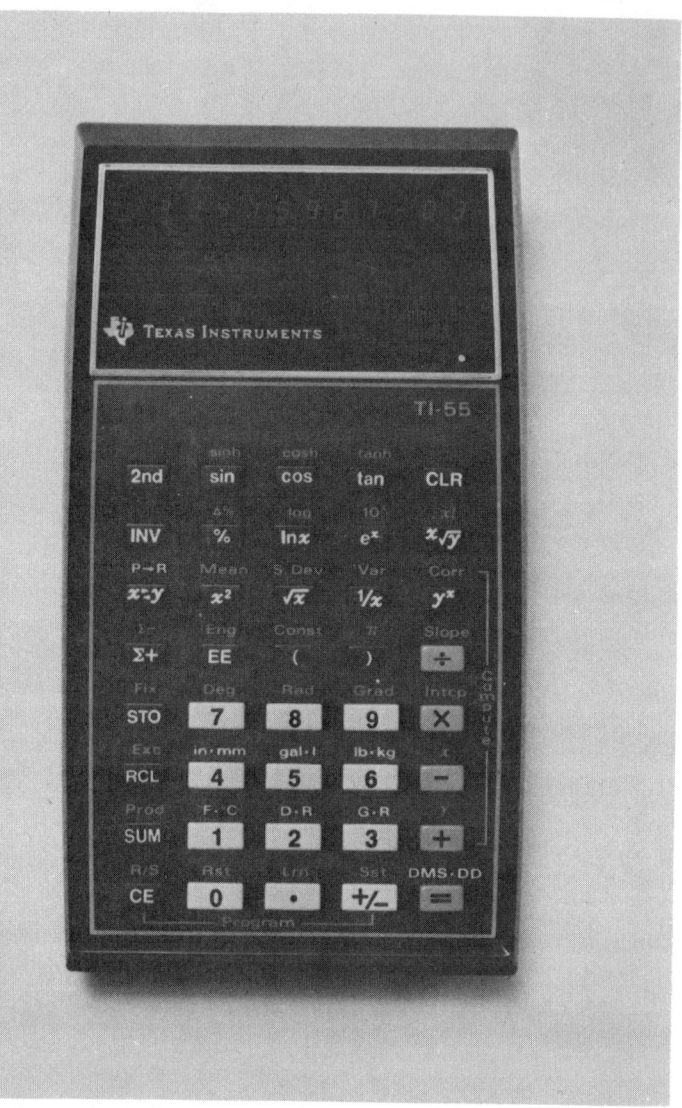

Figure 2-2. Texas Instruments Model TI-55. An advanced scientific calculator with 10 memories, a wide range of mathematical functions, and keyboard programming capability. A single program of up to 32 steps can be established by the operator and retained in the calculator's program memory while the instrument is on.

Figure 2-3. Hewlett-Packard Model HP-67. Any program of up to 224 steps can be established by the operator and stored permanently on a magnetic strip for use at any time. A series of navigational programs prepared by the manufacturer is available on a "software package" of magnetic strips.

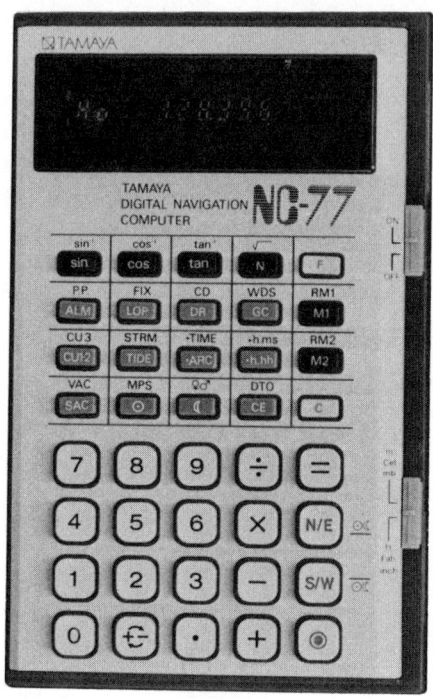

Figure 2-4. Tamaya Model NC-77. Twenty frequently used navigation solutions are prewired into the calculator and are executed from the keyboard. Other problems may be solved manually by using the instrument in the normal calculator mode.

left of the number bank, on the Hewlett-Packard models that employ Reverse Polish Notation.

You should understand the difference between the two logic systems, which manifests itself principally in the order in which the keys for adding, subtracting, multiplying, and dividing are pressed during the solution of a problem. A short example will help to explain. In algebraic logic, a simple arithmetic exercise would be keypunched in the following sequence, [2] [×] [3] [=], and, at the press of the "equals" key, the answer, 6, would appear in the display. In RPN, so-named after the Polish logician who developed the system, the same problem would be solved by pressing [2], then [ENTER↑], to enter it, then [3] [×]. When the "times" sign, [×], is pressed, the answer, 6, is shown in the display. Incidentally, the display is also known as the "X register" in calculator parlance, to distinguish it from the "Y register," which is the working register within the machine.

You can see that for simple problems the number of keystrokes is not materially different. Only in complex exercises, especially those with multiple levels of parentheses, does the difference in logic become significant. In virtually all navigation problems that difference is not of major consequence. It is more important that you are comfortable with the logic you select and develop facility in using it.

Returning to the keyboard, you will find that the special-function keys are almost always clustered at the top, but here the similarity ends. In order to remain within pocket size and still have a keyboard of practical operating dimensions, the physical number of keys is limited, most manufacturers having settled on about thirty-five to forty-five keys. In order to accommodate more functions than there are keys, secondary functions—and in the case of the most powerful models, tertiary functions—are assigned to individual keys. These are brought into use by first pressing a "function change" key, which is identified by various symbols according to the manufacturer's choice. I can only emphasize the requirement that you understand fully

all the functions you have available and the scheme employed for handling multifunction keys on your chosen
instrument.

For example, to convert an angular measurement expressed in degrees, minutes, and seconds (the sexagesimal
system) to degrees and decimal degrees (the decimal system), you could perform the arithmetic operation

$$\text{Degrees} + \left(\frac{\text{Minutes} \times 60 + \text{Seconds}}{3600} \right)$$

by pressing the individual keys in the proper sequence.
Since this is an operation that is repeated frequently in
navigation problems, it is useful to have this special function incorporated in your calculator (see Program A.3).
The Radio Shack EC-495 performs the task with the single
key ⎡ D̄EG ⎤ ; the TI-55 by pressing ⎡ 2nd ⎤ ⎡DMS·DD⎤ (the last
being the secondary function shown above the "equals"
key, ⎡ = ⎤); the HP-67 by pressing ⎡ g ⎤ ⎡H⇌H.MS⎤ (the tertiary function found below the ⎡ 3 ⎤ key); while the NC-77
requires pressing only the primary function key, ⎡ ▶h.hh ⎤.

For the sake of clarity and consistency in the programs
presented in the succeeding chapters, all of the keystroke
sequences are based on the TI-55 style keyboard (Figure
2-2), utilizing algebraic logic. To minimize confusion, the
key symbol shown immediately following the secondary
function key (in this instrument ⎡ 2nd ⎤), will represent the
secondary function, which appears on the keyboard above
the key, rather than the symbol on the face of the key
itself. To illustrate, the symbol ⎡ $x \rightleftarrows y$ ⎤, *not* preceded by the
secondary function key ⎡ 2nd ⎤ in one of our programs, is
understood to call for the *primary* function of the register-
exchange key (exchanging the values in the X and Y registers). If, on the other hand, the symbols ⎡ 2nd ⎤ ⎡P→R⎤ are
shown in a sequence, the *secondary* function of the register-exchange key (changing coordinates from Polar to
Rectangular form), appearing above the key as P→R, is
the one utilized in the program.

Another point to note is the use of the key marked INV on the TI-55 keyboard. That symbol in a program indicates that the primary or secondary function that follows is being called on to perform in the *reverse.* Thus, pressing INV 2nd and the register-exchange key calls for changing Rectangular coordinates back to Polar—the reverse of the operation previously described. To avoid confusion, however, I have arbitrarily adopted the procedure of showing a sequence like this in the form INV 2nd P→R, listing the primary or secondary function *as it appears on the keyboard,* although it is understood that after INV you are utilizing the listed function in *inverse* form.

Remember that the procedure for employing a secondary (or tertiary) function often varies according to the individual manufacturer's keyboard design. Since these alternate functions are used frequently in solving navigation problems, it is to your interest to develop fluency in their use. The extent to which you can take advantage of all the features of your instrument will affect the rapidity and ease with which you can solve problems.

Regardless of the keyboard involved, the solution of any problem on a calculator is set up by identifying the appropriate mathematical formula and then, according to the form of logic used by your instrument, establishing a keypunch sequence, or "program," to solve it. I should point out that there is sometimes more than one formula that can be applied, or more than one keystroke sequence capable of solving a given formula. This is particularly true in some of the more complex exercises. In this book, because I have chosen to present them for learning purposes in a form suitable for a manual calculator, the programs have been set up to be executed in the fewest possible steps or in a sequence to make them most understandable. As you develop facility with a particular instrument, you may be able to reduce the steps still further or otherwise make improvements that utilize your instrument's special capabilities. That's half the fun of experimenting with these marvelous little devices.

As you work your way up to the more advanced calculators, you may wish to adapt these programs to your model —recasting the sequence, for example, if you are going to shift from algebraic logic to Reverse Polish. You will undoubtedly become interested in tackling other types of problems to solve on your calculator. This can be accomplished by acquiring preestablished programs from the manufacturer of your instrument or, most interesting of all, by creating your own programs. More will be said about this in the last chapter.

In connection with the programs presented here, another arbitrary convention—that of signs—has been adopted. North latitudes and East longitudes are considered as positive values; South latitudes and West longitudes carry a minus sign. In the celestial navigation programs, intercepts that are "toward" are considered to be labeled +, while intercepts "away" are negative. Positive or negative signs applying to the display after the calculation of computed altitudes are only to indicate how the rules for changing azimuth angle to true azimuth are to be put to use; the value itself is normally positive. Courses which appear in the display with a negative prefix require the addition of 360°. It isn't necessary to memorize all this now; the use of signs in the individual programs and examples should be quite obvious, and after a short time you'll be using the proper signs automatically.

In most cases, our navigational programs are presented in terms of a practical example and its solution, with the entries suitably identified. To perform other, similar solutions, you need only substitute the appropriate entering values, using the proper signs where called for, and step through the sequence to display the correct answer. In this way, this text can also serve as a reference when you wish to solve an infrequently encountered navigation problem.

In some of the hard-wired, specialized navigational calculators, as well as in some of the program libraries offered with the more sophisticated, programmable machines, certain of the astronomical data used in celestial navigation are incorporated, thus reducing, if not eliminating, the need for an almanac. The *Nautical Almanac* is so easy to use, however, that for the celestial programs in this text, I have elected to utilize the data from that source.

If, as an astronomy or mathematics buff, you feel short-changed by this, you may wish to obtain the *Almanac for Computers,* published by the Nautical Almanac Office of the United States Naval Observatory. Instead of the familiar tabulations, this almanac presents the astronomical data in the form of polynomial series, valid for prescribed time spans. The difficulty is that some of the series are quite involved, even though only representational of the fundamental equations of celestial mechanics that are used for the *American Ephemeris,* from which the *Nautical Almanac* is subtabulated, and which themselves are far too cumbersome for practical use with a hand-held calculator. The navigation section does contain fairly short representations of the Greenwich Hour Angle and declination of the sun, moon, and planets, as well as the GHA of Aries, to a precision of ±0.1 minutes, so if you want to use your calculator only, and have the mathematical background to make use of the information, that is your source.

3. Arithmetic Solutions

The most elementary of the problems in navigation require solution by the application of one or more of the four arithmetic functions, ⌞ + ⌟ ⌞ − ⌟ ⌞ × ⌟ ⌞ ÷ ⌟. In this chapter, common navigational exercises in this category will be discussed, and, in keeping with our format, the solutions will be presented in terms of suggested program sequences based on the TI-55 type algebraic logic keyboard (Figure 2-2).

A.1 Arithmetic Conversions

Let's start with a fundamental navigation problem, using nautical charts for our example. Charted depths may be expressed in feet or fathoms, or, as metrication advances, in meters. Suppose, for example, you wanted to convert, by means of your calculator, a sounding appearing on the chart in either of the latter two forms to its equivalent in feet. Knowing the mathematical relationship by definition—1 fathom = 6 feet; 1 foot = .3048 meters —the conversion is a straightforward exercise in multiplication or division. *Feet* will equal six times *fathoms,* or *meters* divided by .3048 equals *feet.*

Turning to the calculator, for a charted depth of 8 *fathoms,* the sequence to determine *feet* would be ⌷ 8 ⌷ ⌷ × ⌷ ⌷ 6 ⌷ ⌷ = ⌷ and, at the press of the "equals" key, the answer, 48, would appear in the display. If the sounding had read 8 *meters,* you would press ⌷ 8 ⌷ ⌷ ÷ ⌷ ⌷ . ⌷ ⌷ 3 ⌷ ⌷ 0 ⌷ ⌷ 4 ⌷ ⌷ 8 ⌷ ⌷ = ⌷ to derive the answer, 26.2467, or for practical purposes, 26.2 *feet.*

Don't proceed until you have this type of exercise with your calculator down pat.

A.2 Time-Speed-Distance

Another common problem for the navigator, and a good one on which to practice your basic calculator technique, is the relationship between time, speed, and distance. The arithmetical formula for solving these problems is, *"Time times Speed equals Distance."* Given any two of the quantities you can solve for the third. Thus, *Distance* divided by *Speed* equals *Time,* or *Distance* divided by *Time* equals *Speed,* and so forth.

As a practical exercise, let's see how far you will go in 2 hours at 3 knots. The calculator is punched ⌷ 2 ⌷ ⌷ × ⌷ ⌷ 3 ⌷ ⌷ = ⌷, and the answer is displayed—6 nautical miles.

Answering the question, "How long will it take to go 17.5 miles at 5 knots?" the sequence would be ⌷ 1 ⌷ ⌷ 7 ⌷ ⌷ . ⌷ ⌷ 5 ⌷ ⌷ ÷ ⌷ ⌷ 5 ⌷ ⌷ = ⌷, and the final figure appearing in the X register or display, 3.5, is the solution expressed in hours. Knots, of course, mean nautical miles per hour.

Fuel consumption and similar problems for which a direct arithmetical relationship can be preestablished, are worked with the same type of keyboard sequence, and very quickly and easily even though the numbers, or their decimal parts, may be large.

A.3 Time/Arc Decimal Conversions

Most of us are accustomed to working with the decimal system, and our usual arithmetic computations are made in that mode. In navigational operations, however, time (expressed in hours, minutes, and seconds) and arc (degrees, minutes, and seconds) utilize a system called "sexagesimal," in which 60 seconds equal a minute and 60 minutes equal an hour or degree.

In our second time-speed-distance example (Program A.2), the decimal answer, you will recall, was 3.5 hours. Suppose you want to express this in hours and minutes? You can, of course, multiply the decimal hours by 60 to obtain minutes, and any decimal minutes by 60 to figure seconds. But this, as discussed in Chapter 2, is cumbersome, and many scientific calculators provide a built-in conversion function that transforms a time or arc measurement expressed in hours or degrees, minutes, and seconds to its decimal equivalent, or vice versa, with just two or three keystrokes.

A typical calculator routine, and one used frequently in the examples in this text, is to enter the time, or arc, in the sexagesimal mode in the form, hours (or degrees), *decimal point,* minutes, and seconds, press the conversion keys, and read the answer in the decimal format. In the reverse, enter with the decimal form, call on the inverse function, and read the sexagesimal notation directly. In the example under discussion, the sequence would be the reverse one and the keys pressed on the TI-55 would be ⬚ 3 ⬚ ⬚ · ⬚ ⬚ 5 ⬚ ⬚ INV ⬚ ⬚ 2nd ⬚ ⬚DMS·DD⬚, displaying the answer, 3 hours, 30 minutes, and no seconds, in the form, 3.3 (or, if four decimal places were displayed, 3.3000).

Let's take another example. Nine hours, 14 minutes, and 42 seconds is keyed in as follows: ⬚ 9 ⬚ ⬚ · ⬚ ⬚ 1 ⬚ ⬚ 4 ⬚ ⬚ 4 ⬚ ⬚ 2 ⬚, and when ⬚ 2nd ⬚ ⬚DMS·DD⬚ is pressed, the display, 9.245, represents the time in hours and decimal

parts. Conversely, entering with 152.2° and pressing
[INV] [2nd] [DMS·DD]—the reverse conversion on this keyboard—the answer, 152°12'00", is displayed in the form,
152.12. This is a system used by many calculators, the first
two digits to the right of the decimal point in the sexagesimal form indicating minutes, and the next two, the seconds. Familiarize yourself with the conversion technique
on your instrument since you will be calling on it often.

In celestial navigation, it is common to indicate arc
measurements in the form, degrees, minutes, and *tenths*
of minutes (rather than in seconds)—a slight further com-
plication. With all but the specialized navigational calculators that have been prewired to accept that form, it is
usually simplest to express the tenths of minutes as seconds by mentally multiplying the decimal figure by 6. In
the reverse operation, the seconds can be converted to
tenths of minutes by dividing by 6. Fifteen point 6 minutes
thus becomes 15'36", while 10 minutes, 24 seconds equals
10.4 minutes of arc. In all of our celestial examples you
will notice that the calculator accepts and displays minutes and seconds although the problem or the solution
may be expressed in minutes and tenths—that conversion
having been handled mentally. Don't confuse this, however, with the conversion of the sexagesimal expression
into hours and decimal hours, or degrees and decimal degrees, which is the form in which the arithmetical computation must be carried out by the calculator.

A.4 Sexagesimal Arithmetic

There are a number of cases in navigation where arithmetic computations are required to be made with figures
expressed in the sexagesimal system. A common instance
in celestial navigation is in adding or subtracting incre-
ments of arc. For example, if the Greenwich Hour Angle
of the sun for 16 hours is 60°52.0', and the increment for 35
minutes and 8 seconds is 8°47.0', what is the total GHA at
16h35m08s, the time of the observation?

The calculator procedure is to change each value to degrees and decimal degrees, perform the addition, and convert the answer back to the sexagesimal form. The sequence for the particular keyboard we are using would be:

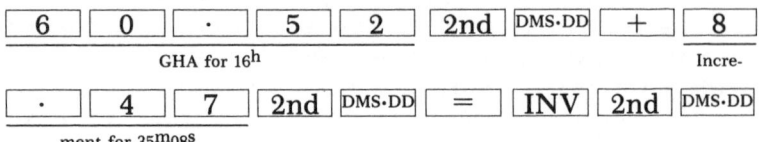

GHA for 16^h Incre-

ment for 35^{m}08^s

The answer, 69°39', is displayed after the last keypunch as 69.39. Some advanced calculators are equipped with a special key to perform addition or subtraction of sexagesimal expressions and to display the answer in that mode without having to make the individual conversions and final reconversion. The keyboard that this text uses for demonstrating, however, does not have that feature.

Another typical exercise in sexagesimal arithmetic is the determination of ETA (Estimated Time of Arrival). This combines time-speed-distance arithmetic with sexagesimal/decimal conversion. For example, departing at 2:15 in the morning (0215), a vessel expects to proceed at 5 knots to its destination 17.5 miles away. At what time does the navigator expect to arrive?

First, solving for the elapsed time of the run, the sequence is pressed, 1 7 . 5 ÷ 5 =, and the answer, 3.5 hours, is displayed. Next, the starting time is entered, converted to decimal hours by pressing 2 . 1 5 2nd DMS·DD and that figure added to the elapsed time to produce the estimated time of arrival. Since that result will be in the decimal form, the final step is to reconvert it to the sexagesimal system in order to express the ETA as watch time. As a continuous program, the keystroke sequence would be:

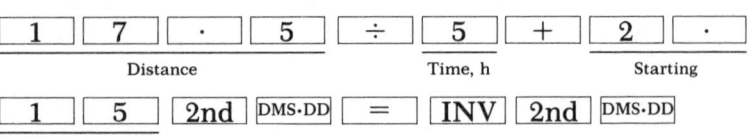

Distance   Time, h   Starting

time, h.m

The answer, displayed as 5.45, indicates that the ETA will be 0545, or 5:45 a.m.

A.5 Time of Sunrise, Sunset, Twilight

The navigator may wish from time to time to precalculate the local or zone time of the rising and setting phenomena, or of twilight itself in order to plan his morning or evening observations.

As an example, the *Nautical Almanac* indicates that sunset at Latitude 40° North on May 8, 1979, will occur at 1901. What time will it occur on that date at the vessel's estimated position, Latitude 40° North, Longitude 72° West?

Recognizing that the almanac times are, for practical purposes, equivalent to the zone time at *any* standard meridian (the standard, or "zone" meridian, is the nearest one exactly divisible by 15), it is necessary to convert the difference in longitude between the vessel's position and its standard meridian to a difference in time (15° of arc = 1 hour of time) and to apply that correction to the tabular time. Following this procedure, the calculator program to solve our example would be:

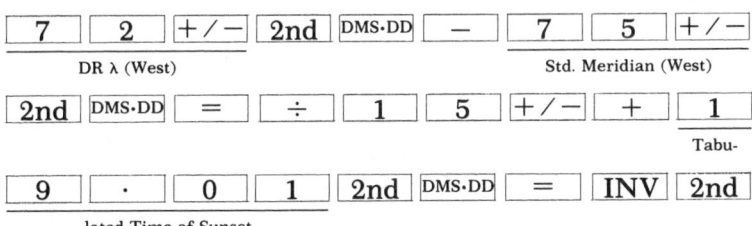

DMS·DD   The final display indicates the time of the phenomenon, 1849, as it occurs at 72° West longitude, in terms of the local zone time. In extracting the published time from the *Nautical Almanac,* if the position of the vessel is at a latitude between those tabulated, a simple interpolation by eye will usually suffice. Otherwise, the degrees of latitude from the nearest one tabulated, divided by the number of degrees difference between successive tabulations (usually 10 degrees), multiplied by the minutes of difference between the respective tabulated times, will yield the correction in minutes. Inspection will tell you which way to apply it.

You will notice in this keyboard sequence that the degrees of longitude in the first two entries (DR λ and zone meridian) were transformed by the ⎡2nd⎤ ⎡DMS·DD⎤ keys into degrees and decimals. Strictly speaking, since in this instance the values were in whole degrees, that conversion step could have been omitted. It was included here so that you can use the same sequence with values entered as degrees, minutes, and seconds if you wish. Notice also the use of the sign-change key ⎡+/−⎤ to make the displayed value negative as is our convention for West longitudes.

A.6 Distance to Horizon

The navigator may be called upon to determine the distance to his visible horizon from the elevation of his viewpoint, or "height of eye." This exercise is useful for deciding whether or not there is a true horizon for making celestial observations when land or haze intervenes, or for estimating the "visibility" of objects of known height—the distance from which they can be seen at sea. The formula is a simple one:

$$\text{Horizon distance in nautical miles} = 1.144 \sqrt{\text{Height of eye, feet}}$$

The calculator program is equally straightforward, utilizing the instrument's square root function. For example, what is the distance to the horizon for an observer whose height of eye is 15 feet? The program, ⎡1⎤ ⎡·⎤ ⎡1⎤ ⎡4⎤ ⎡4⎤ ⎡×⎤ ⎡1⎤ ⎡5⎤ ⎡√x⎤ ⎡=⎤, produces the answer, 4.43 nautical miles.

Should there be an object beyond the horizon whose height is, say, 100 feet, *its* distance to the horizon calculated in a similar manner would be 11.44 miles. Then its distance, added to the distance to the observer's horizon, produces the maximum range (15.87 nautical miles) at which any part of the object can be seen from the 15-foot height of eye.

A.7 Sextant Corrections

There are three principal corrections that have to be made to an altitude as measured by sextant (hs) to obtain the "Observed Altitude" (Ho) that is used in a celestial sight solution.

The first two adjustments, Index Correction and Dip, are determined and added algebraically to the Sextant Altitude to produce an intermediate value called "Apparent Altitude" (ha). The Index Correction is found by making an observation of the horizon with the sextant to determine the error, if any, in the index. It will usually be a small number of minutes or fractions of a minute, and either positive or negative. Dip, which is the angle between the true horizontal and the observer's line of sight to the horizon, can be calculated by the formula:

$$\text{Dip, in minutes of arc} = 0.97 \sqrt{\text{Height of eye, feet}}$$

or from the inspection tables inside the cover of the *Nautical Almanac*. The value of the Dip Correction is always negative.

To apply the first two corrections by calculator it is necessary to change each value to decimal form, add them algebraically, and return the answer to the sexagesimal expression. As an example, what would the Apparent Altitude be after correcting a Sextant Altitude of 45°21.5′ for an I.C. of +1.4′ and a height of eye of 15.4 feet? Starting with the Dip, the keystroke sequence would be, ☐1☐ ☐5☐ ☐·☐ ☐4☐ ☐√x̄☐ ☐×☐ ☐·☐ ☐9☐ ☐7☐ ☐=☐, displaying the Dip Correction, (−) 3.8′. Then the entire program can be run in order as follows:

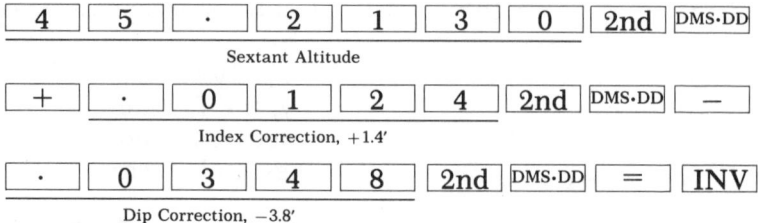

4	5	.	2	1	3	0	2nd	DMS·DD

Sextant Altitude

+	.	0	1	2	4	2nd	DMS·DD	—

Index Correction, +1.4'

.	0	3	4	8	2nd	DMS·DD	=	INV

Dip Correction, −3.8'

2nd DMS·DD , producing the answer, 45°19′06″, or, if you prefer, 45°19.1′, the Apparent Altitude (ha).

You will note in this exercise that the original values expressed in minutes and tenths were transformed mentally and entered in the form, degrees, *decimal point,* minutes, and seconds, and then changed to decimal degrees on the calculator before the arithmetic was performed. At the conclusion of the program, the answer was displayed in sexagesimal form, which can be restated in degrees, minutes, and tenths, if desired, by the reverse mental process. For clarity, the Dip calculation was made separately and entered in the normal order, but it would have been perfectly correct to apply the negative sign to the value computed and to add the Sextant Altitude and Index Correction to it. The result would have been the same. You will discover in many programs that the order in which the variables are entered is not inviolable, although application of the proper signs, positive or negative, always is.

Repeat this exercise until you understand it thoroughly, as it is a typical example of the sexagesimal algebraic addition made in numerous cases in celestial navigation computations.

Apparent Altitude (ha) is used for obtaining the third, or "Refraction," Correction, which is found for the sun, stars and planets inside the front cover of the *Nautical Almanac,* and for the moon, in two parts, inside the back cover. The second of the moon's corrections also requires the horizontal parallax value, which is found on the *Almanac*'s daily pages.

The Refraction Correction is applied according to its sign to the Apparent Altitude to obtain the Observed Altitude (Ho). On the calculator this can be accomplished by leaving the Apparent Altitude in decimal form at the "equals" sign (after the ⌑ = ⌑ key is pressed in the previous sequence), adding, algebraically, the Refraction Correction—also expressed in decimal degrees—and converting the sum back to the sexagesimal form at the conclusion.

The refraction corrections given in the *Almanac* tables are based on a surface temperature of 50° F (10° C) and an atmospheric pressure of 29.33 inches (1010 millibars). Should conditions vary significantly from these standards, a small additional correction may be found in the *Nautical Almanac* Table A4, which is included in the calculator arithmetic in the same way as all the others. It is, however, seldom called for in normal yachting weather.

Refraction can also be determined directly by calculator by the following formula:

$$\text{Refraction Correction, in decimal degrees} = \frac{0.97 \tan(ha - \tan^{-1}12\,[ha + 3°])}{60}$$

where ha is the Apparent Altitude expressed in decimal degrees.

This formula may be useful if you are programming a calculator to perform the sextant corrections automatically, as it produces the answer, with the proper negative sign, in convenient form for combining with the rest of the program. On a manual calculator, however, using the formula is much more involved than using the *Almanac* tables, the quickest and simplest approach. The use of trigonometric functions on a calculator, which this formula requires, is explained in Chapter 5.

A.8 Time of Local Apparent Noon

One of the classic exercises in celestial navigation, and one of the easiest to perform, is the determination of latitude from the altitude of the sun at Local Apparent Noon —that moment when the sun's path crosses the meridian of the observer and attains its highest altitude for the day. The Greenwich Hour Angle of the sun and the longitude (λ) of the observer at that instant are the same if the longitude is West (or 360°−λ if East), making the Local Hour Angle zero. The procedure for determining latitude in this special case is contained in the next program, A.9, but first the navigator needs to estimate the time at which LAN will occur so that he can schedule his arrival on deck to start taking a series of sights shortly before the maximum altitude is expected.

The object of this program is the calculation of the time of LAN. It has been figured in terms of Greenwich Mean Time (GMT), since you will want that form to enter the *Almanac* for the declination information in the subsequent latitude computation. You can adjust to the local zone time by mentally adding or subtracting the number of hours your time zone is fast or slow of Greenwich.

The program steps, which are a combination of degree and decimal conversions and arithmetic, start by your entering an estimate of your noon longitude (directly, if West, or 360°−λ, if East) and converting that longitude to decimal degrees. From that figure is subtracted the next *smaller* value for the sun's GHA from the sun column in the daily pages of the *Almanac* for your (Greenwich) date; converting the GHA to decimal degrees, of course, before making the subtraction. At this juncture, incidentally, you can also note and record the declination value alongside the GHA for use in the latitude calculation later.

The difference in arc between the sun's next smaller GHA from the table and the observer's estimated longitude is divided by 15 to convert it to decimal hours. That figure is further transformed by the use of the INV 2nd DMS·DD routine to express the difference as minutes and seconds of time. The Greenwich Mean Time of LAN, then, will be the hours opposite the GHA selected in the *Almanac,* and the minutes and seconds from the calculation.

Let me demonstrate this sequence with an example. On June 9, 1979, a navigator estimates his longitude at the approximate time of LAN to be 65°45.0′ W. The next smaller value in the sun's GHA column in the *Nautical Almanac,* on June 9, is 60°13.6′ at 16 hours GMT (see Figure 3-1). What is the estimated time of LAN?

JUNE 9, 1979		
G.M.T.	**SUN**	
	G.H.A.	Dec.
d h	° ′	° ′
9 00	180 15.5	N22 51.6
01	195 15.4	51.8
02	210 15.2	52.0
03	225 15.1 ··	52.3
04	240 15.0	52.5
05	255 14.9	52.7
06	270 14.8	N22 52.9
07	285 14.6	53.1
S 08	300 14.5	53.4
A 09	315 14.4 ··	53.6
T 10	330 14.3	53.8
U 11	345 14.2	54.0
R 12	0 14.0	N22 54.2
D 13	15 13.9	54.4
A 14	30 13.8	54.6
Y 15	45 13.7 ··	54.8
16	60 13.6	55.1
17	75 13.4	55.3
18	90 13.3	N22 55.5
19	105 13.2	55.7
20	120 13.1	55.9
21	135 13.0 ··	56.1
22	150 12.8	56.3
23	165 12.7	56.5

Figure 3-1. Excerpt from SUN column, Nautical Almanac, *June 9, 1979.*

The calculator keypunch sequence is as follows:

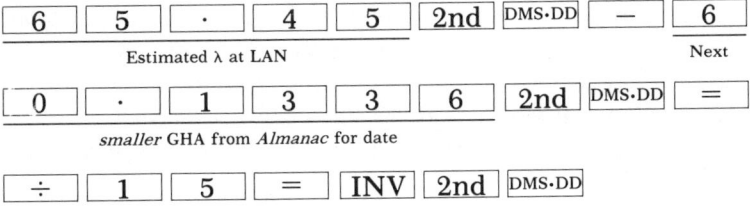

| 6 | 5 | · | 4 | 5 | 2nd | DMS·DD | − | 6 |

Estimated λ at LAN   Next

| 0 | · | 1 | 3 | 3 | 6 | 2nd | DMS·DD | = |

smaller GHA from *Almanac* for date

| ÷ | 1 | 5 | = | INV | 2nd | DMS·DD |

The answer, displayed as .2205 reads, "22 minutes, 05 seconds," which, when appended to the hours of GMT (16ʰ) corresponding to the sun's GHA value selected, produces the Greenwich Mean Time of 16ʰ22ᵐ05ˢ as the estimated time of LAN. Since the vessel is in the time zone four hours slow of Greenwich, the local time of LAN would be 12-22-05. You should note in this program that because we are dealing with differences measured in a westerly direction, we have departed from our usual convention of signs. The longitude, in this case, is always dealt with as a positive value.

Another popular way to approximate the time of LAN in terms of local time is to take the listing for the time of Meridian Passage (Figure 3-2) from the daily pages of the *Nautical Almanac* for the proper (Greenwich) date and adjust it by the difference between the estimated longitude of the observer and the nearest standard, or "zone" meridian expressed in time (just as you did in Program A.5). Since 15 degrees of longitude is equal to one hour of time, 4 minutes of time are the equivalent of one degree of longitude, and 4 seconds of time equal to one minute of arc. Positions to the east of the standard meridian will experience earlier occurrence of LAN, while those to the west will find it later.

Day	SUN Eqn. of Time 00ʰ	12ʰ	Mer. Pass.
	m s	m s	h m
9	01 02	00 56	11 59
10	00 51	00 45	11 59
11	00 39	00 33	11 59

Figure 3-2. Equation of Time and Time of Meridian Passage from Nautical Almanac *for June 9, 1979.*

Returning to the practical example, the time of the sun's Meridian Passage, as shown in the *Almanac* for June 9, 1979, is 1159. The vessel's position is west of the nearest standard meridian (at 60°W), making LAN *later* than the listed time. Running this on the calculator, the program is as follows:

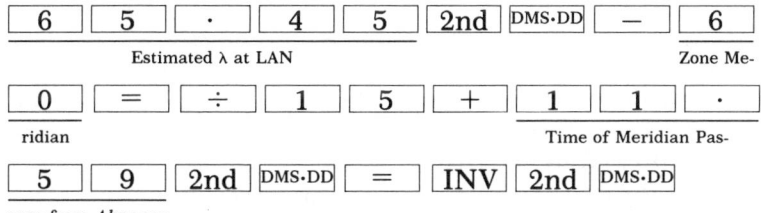

Estimated λ at LAN

ridian

Time of Meridian Pas-

sage from *Almanac*

The answer displayed, 1222, is the approximate time of
LAN expressed as local time. It is close to, but not quite as
precise as the first method, since the Meridian Passage
listed in the *Almanac* is only given to the nearest minute.
It is, however, adequate for planning your LAN observation. In this program you will also notice that as the standard meridian (60°) is expressed in whole degrees, the conversion to decimal degrees was not necessary.

Still another method, yielding precision to seconds,
utilizes the Equation of Time (for 12^h) that also appears
in the *Nautical Almanac* (see Figure 3-2). On the same
June 9, for example, the Equation of Time was noted to be
00^m56^s. The formula for this method of solution is:

GMT of LAN = Estimated longitude $\div$ 15 + 12 $\pm$ Equation of Time

the last value being subtractive if the Meridian Passage
occurs before noon and additive if after. The longitude
used is expressed positively and is the estimated longitude
if West, or $360° - λ$ if East. For our same practical example,
the calculator would be keyed as follows:

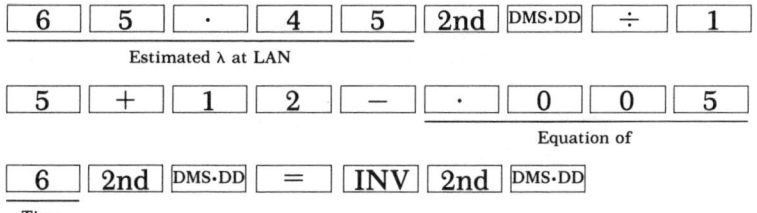

Estimated λ at LAN

Equation of

Time

The answer displayed, 16-22-04 (GMT), compares closely with the first calculator method, which I personally prefer since it requires one less step, avoids the question as to whether to add or subtract the Equation of Time, and enables the sun's declination to be extracted at the same time as the next smaller GHA.

In any of these methods, if the time calculated for LAN is quite different from that you used in selecting the estimated longitude, the longitude should be reestimated to correspond more closely with the calculated time, and the program rerun with the improved longitude estimate.

A.9 Position by Meridian Transit—Noon Sight

The "noon sight," which is an observation of the sun's altitude at the time of upper meridian transit (Local Apparent Noon), is both an ancient tradition and an easy calculator exercise, requiring only sexagesimal/decimal conversions and simple arithmetic.

The procedure for solving a noon sight for latitude is accomplished in five steps:

• Correct the Sextant Altitude (hs) to obtain the Observed Altitude (Ho). (See Program A.7.)
• Subtract Ho from 90°, noting the sun's bearing, N or S, and identify the difference (z) with a negative sign if the sun bore *North.*
• Enter the sun's declination for the GMT of LAN (see Program A.8), marking it negative if *South.*
• Add z and declination.
• The answer will be the latitude, North if positive, South if negative.

Let's look at two examples to illustrate these steps. The Observed Altitude of the sun on the meridian, bearing South, is 49°27.0′. The declination at the approximate time of LAN is 17°59.0′ S. What is the latitude? The keystroke sequence starts as follows:

| 9 | 0 | − | 4 | 9 | · | 2 | 7 | 2nd |

Observed Altitude, Ho

DMS·DD ☐ = ☐ , and since the sun's bearing is South, the program continues *without* changing the sign of the value in the display to negative: ☐ + ☐ ☐ 1 ☐ ☐ 7 ☐ ☐ · ☐ ☐ 5 ☐

Decli-

☐ 9 ☐ ☐+ / −☐ ☐ 2nd ☐ DMS·DD ☐ = ☐ ☐ INV ☐ ☐ 2nd ☐ DMS·DD

nation (South)

The answer shown is the latitude, 22°34.0′ *North* (because the sign was positive).

Suppose the Ho had been 80°21.0′ and the sun bore *North,* while the declination was 8°50.0′N. Then the program would require changing the sign to negative after the first subtraction and would look like this:

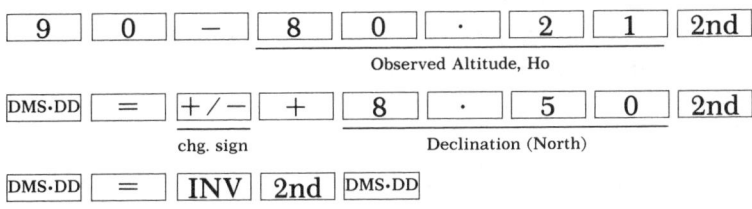

☐ 9 ☐ ☐ 0 ☐ ☐ − ☐ ☐ 8 ☐ ☐ 0 ☐ ☐ · ☐ ☐ 2 ☐ ☐ 1 ☐ ☐ 2nd ☐

Observed Altitude, Ho

DMS·DD ☐ = ☐ ☐+ / −☐ ☐ + ☐ ☐ 8 ☐ ☐ · ☐ ☐ 5 ☐ ☐ 0 ☐ ☐ 2nd ☐

chg. sign   Declination (North)

DMS·DD ☐ = ☐ ☐ INV ☐ ☐ 2nd ☐ DMS·DD

The final display shows the latitude, 0°49.0′, and it would be *South* because the sign is negative.

Since, as it was pointed out in Program A.8, the Local Hour Angle of the sun is zero at the time of LAN, it follows that if you can determine the exact GMT of the Meridian Passage, you could find the corresponding GHA for that time in the *Almanac* and it would be equal to your longitude West of Greenwich (or 360° − λ if East). The practical problem here is determining the *exact* time of the Meridian Passage. If the precise moment at which the sun bore exactly North or South, or the instant the sun attained its highest altitude, could be determined with accuracy, this solution for longitude would be simple. Unfortunately, sufficiently accurate azimuths are almost impossible to obtain at sea, so the altitude method is the only one attempted. The most practical approach is to make a series of observations both before and after the Meridian Passage, trying, to the extent possible, to pair up altitudes observed during the sun's ascendancy with corresponding readings after the maximum altitude has passed. Then, by plotting all the sextant readings against time on a graph, you may be able to come reasonably close to the correct time of LAN, although it is not easy.

The calculator program, on the other hand, is quite simple. The sun's GHA for the hour of GMT is taken from the SUN column in the daily pages of the *Nautical Almanac,* transformed to decimal degrees and added to the increment for minutes and seconds (the increment having been taken from the *Almanac* or calculated by multiplying the minutes and seconds of time, expressed in decimal hours, by the hourly increase in the sun's GHA, 15°).

For example, given an exact time of LAN on June 9, 1979, of 16h22m05s GMT, what is the observer's longitude? In the *Almanac* (Figure 3-1), we find that the sun's GHA at 16 hours on that date is 60°13.6′. The calculator program, following the steps outlined, then looks like this:

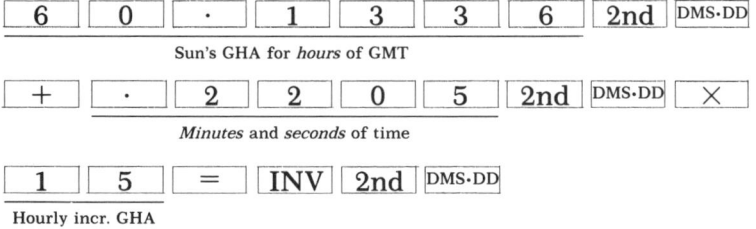

The answer, 65°44′51″, or 65°44.8′, is expressed as West longitude. Had it been greater than 180°, the value displayed should be subtracted from 360° to read East longitude.

Although the data in this sequence are entered in the order given, the incremental minutes and seconds of time, converted to decimal hours, are actually multiplied in the calculation by 15 degrees (the sun's hourly increase in GHA) *before* the addition is performed with the tabular GHA. The TI-55 calculator has the feature of automatically following the classic rule of mathematical hierarchy, "Multiplication and division before addition and subtraction." In models that don't have this feature, use may be made of the parentheses keys to insure performing the operations in the proper order.

POLARIS (POLE STAR) TABLES, 1979
FOR DETERMINING LATITUDE FROM SEXTANT ALTITUDE AND FOR AZIMUTH

L.H.A. ARIES	120°– 129°	130°– 139°	140°– 149°	150°– 159°	160°– 169°	170°– 179°	180°– 189°	190°– 199°	200°– 209°	210°– 219°	220°– 229°	230°– 239°
	a_0	a_0	a_0	a_0	a_0	a_0	a_0	a_0	a_0	a_0	a_0	a_0
0	0 56·7	1 05·3	1 13·8	1 21·8	1 29·1	1 35·4	1 40·7	1 44·7	1 47·4	1 48·5	1 48·2	1 46·5
1	57·5	06·2	14·6	22·5	29·7	36·0	41·2	45·0	47·5	48·6	48·1	46·2
2	58·4	07·0	15·4	23·3	30·4	36·6	41·6	45·4	47·7	48·6	48·0	45·9
3	0 59·3	07·9	16·2	24·0	31·1	37·1	42·0	45·7	47·9	48·6	47·9	45·6
4	1 00·1	08·7	17·0	24·8	31·7	37·7	42·5	45·9	48·0	48·6	47·7	45·3
5	1 01·0	1 09·6	1 17·9	1 25·5	1 32·4	1 38·2	1· 42·9	1 46·2	1 48·1	1 48·6	1 47·5	1 45·0
6	01·9	10·4	18·6	26·2	33·0	38·7	43·3	46·5	48·2	48·5	47·3	44·7
7	02·7	11·3	19·4	27·0	33·6	·39·3	43·7	46·7	48·3	48·5	47·1	44·4
8	03·6	12·1	20·2	27·7	34·2	39·8	44·0	46·9	48·4	48·4	46·9	44·0
9	04·5	13·0	21·0	28·4	34·9	40·2	44·4	47·2	48·5	48·3	46·7	43·6
10	1 05·3	1 13·8	1 21·8	1 29·1	1 35·4	1 40·7	1 44·7	1 47·4	1 48·5	1 48·2	1 46·5	1 43·2
Lat.	a_1	a_1	a_1	a_1	a_1	a_1	a_1	a_1	a_1	a_1	a_1	a_1
0	0·2	0·2	0·2	0·3	0·4	0·4	0·5	0·6	0·6	0·6	0·6	0·5
10	·2	·2	·3	·3	·4	·5	·5	·6	·6	·6	·6	·5
20	·3	·3	·3	·4	·4	·5	·5	·6	·6	·6	·6	·6
30	·4	·4	·4	·4	·5	·5	·6	·6	·6	·6	·6	·6
40	0·5	0·5	0·5	0·5	0·5	0·6	0·6	0·6	0·6	0·6	0·6	0·6
45	·5	·5	·5	·6	·6	·6	·6	·6	·6	·6	·6	·6
50	·6	·6	·6	·6	·6	·6	·6	·6	·6	·6	·6	·6
55	·7	·7	·7	·7	·6	·6	·6	·6	·6	·6	·6	·6
60	·8	·8	·8	·7	·7	·7	·6	·6	·6	·6	·6	·6
62	0·8	0·8	0·8	0·8	0·7	0·7	0·7	0·6	0·6	0·6	0·6	0·6
64	0·9	0·9	·9	·8	·8	·7	·7	·6	·6	·6	·6	·6
66	1·0	1·0	0·9	·9	·8	·7	·7	·6	·6	·6	·6	·7
68	1·1	1·0	1·0	0·9	0·9	0·8	0·7	0·6	0·6	0·6	0·6	0·7
Month	a_2	a_2	a_2	a_2	a_2	a_2	a_2	a_2	a_2	a_2	a_2	a_2
Jan.	0·6	0·6	0·6	0·5	0·5	0·5	0·5	0·5	0·4	0·4	0·4	0·4
Feb.	·8	·7	·7	·7	·6	·6	·5	·5	·5	·4	·4	·4
Mar.	0·9	0·9	0·9	·8	·8	·7	·7	·6	·6	·5	·5	·4
Apr.	1·0	1·0	1·0	0·9	0·9	0·9	0·8	0·8	0·7	0·7	0·6	0·5
May	0·9	1·0	1·0	1·0	1·0	1·0	0·9	0·9	0·9	·8	·7	·7
June	·8	0·9	0·9	1·0	1·0	1·0	1·0	1·0	1·0	0·9	·9	·8
July	0·7	0·7	0·8	0·8	0·9	0·9	0·9	1·0	1·0	1·0	0·9	0·9
Aug.	·5	·6	·6	·7	·7	·8	·8	0·9	0·9	0·9	·9	·9
Sept.	·4	·4	·4	·5	·5	·6	·6	·7	·7	·8	·8	·9
Oct.	0·3	0·3	0·3	0·3	0·4	0·4	0·5	0·5	0·6	0·6	0·7	0·7
Nov.	·3	·2	·2	·2	·2	·3	·3	·3	·4	·4	·5	·6
Dec.	0·3	0·3	0·2	0·2	0·2	0·2	0·2	0·2	0·2	0·3	0·3	0·4

Figure 3-3. Extract of the Polaris Tables from Nautical Almanac.

A.10 Latitude by Polaris

Although it is not employed very frequently, the method of working an observation of Polaris, the Pole Star, is another "shortcut" way of determining latitude—always North, of course, since Polaris is visible only in the Northern Hemisphere.

The steps in the calculator solution are to correct the Sextant Altitude (hs) to the Observed Altitude (Ho) (see Program A.7) and then, entering the Polaris Tables in the back of the *Nautical Almanac* (Figure 3-3), first with the

LHA of Aries at the time of the observation, next with the approximate latitude of the observer, and then with the month, extract the three corrections and apply them according to the formula:

$$Ho + a_0 + a_1 + a_2 - 1° = Latitude$$

Here is a practical example to illustrate the procedure. On April 21, 1979, at GMT 23h18m56s, in longitude 37°14.0′ W, and in the approximate latitude of 50° N, an observation of Polaris (corrected for IC, Dip, and Refraction as in Program A.7) produced an Ho of 49°31.6′. From the daily pages of the *Almanac,* the GHA of Aries was extracted and, by applying the estimated longitude, the LHA of Aries was found to be 161°55.8′. Entering the Polaris Tables (Figure 3-3), the first correction, a_0, was 1°30.4′, a_1 was 0.6′, and a_2, 0.9′. With this information at hand, the calculator sequence goes as follows:

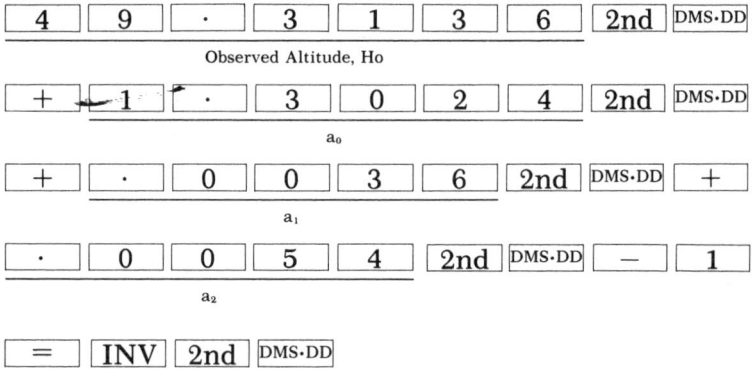

The final display, 50.0330, or 50°03.5′, is the (North) latitude.

Using the *Almanac* this way, this is an instance in which the calculator solution may show little or no time advantage over simple inspection. It will be up to you, and to the facility you develop with your instrument, to decide whether or not, in cases like this, the solution by calculator is really to your benefit.

4. Vector Arithmetic

A branch of mathematics of frequent use to the navigator is vector arithmetic. A vector, simply stated, is a straight line representing direction by its orientation and magnitude by its length. Courses and distances plotted on a chart, or courses and speeds shown on a current triangle, are examples of vectors in everyday use.

Positions located by bearing and distance from a point of origin, or "pole," are said to be located by their "polar coordinates." The identical position can also be located by its distance east or west and its distance north or south of the point of origin. These latter two components are called its "rectangular coordinates." You will see in Figure 4-1 that Point A can be located from Point P *either* by its polar coordinates, Course Angle Cn and Distance D, or by its rectangular coordinates, e and n.

In vector arithmetic, as commonly used in navigational calculations, each vector, expressed in polar form, is converted into its rectangular equivalent, the algebraic sums of the respective E–W and N–S components computed, and the totals reconverted to the polar representation—the form for sailing actual courses at sea. The capability to make this conversion automatically is a most desirable

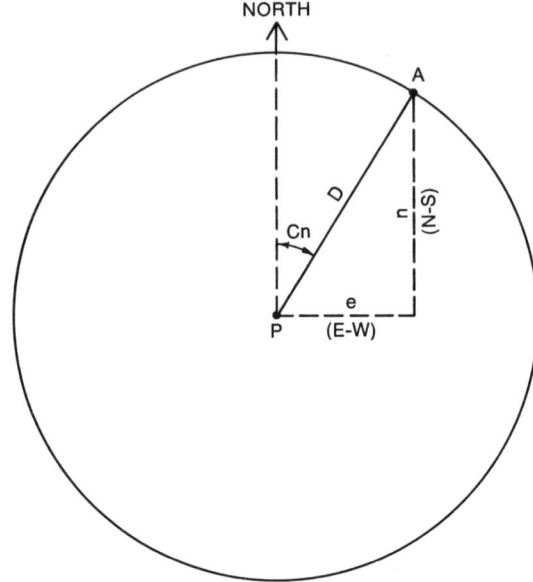

*Figure 4-1. Polar and Rectangular Coordinates—Point
A can be located either by the Course Angle* Cn *and
Distance* D, *or the E–W component* e *and the N–S com-
ponent* n.

feature in a navigational calculator, and the programs to
follow are so conceived.

V.1 Current Sailing—Course and Speed Made Good

In sailing through a current, a vessel will be diverted
from its intended course by the action of the current. But
by how much? That is the question we shall solve by calculator in the next two exercises.

Almost always, the navigator knows the course his vessel is steering and its speed through the water. If he also
knows, or can make a good estimate from tables or obser-

vations, of the direction, or "set," in which the current is
flowing and the rate of flow, or "drift," he can compute the
actual course and speed made good. Figure 4-2 shows, dia-
grammatically, the relationship between the elements of
the current triangle.

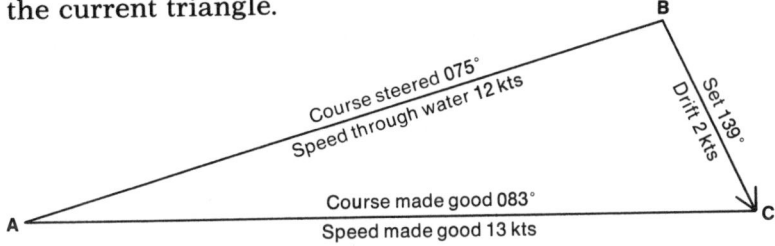

*Figure 4-2. The current triangle illustrating the relation-
ship between its component parts.*

The calculator solution of this type of problem involves
vector arithmetic, and a practical example will serve to
illustrate the procedure. A vessel on Course 075° at 12 knots
sails through a current setting toward 139° with a drift rate
of 2 knots. What is the actual course and speed made good?
   In the program to follow, we will change the polar coordinates of the vessel's and the current's vectors into their
rectangular components, add those components algebraically, and return the sums to the polar mode. New elements to note here are the use of the ⎡STO⎤ key to store a
value in one of the calculator's memory registers and the
⎡RCL⎤ key to recall the contents of the memory to the display. This is a standard way for calculators to retain intermediate data without having to record it and reenter it
when needed.
   This program will also serve to introduce you to the use
of register arithmetic, in which a value displayed in the X
register can be applied at any time to the contents of one
of the addressable memories by employing the primary,
secondary, or inverse function of the ⎡SUM⎤ key followed by
the number of the memory register. You will be meeting
for the first time, too, the register-exchange key, ⎡$x \rightleftarrows y$⎤, the
purpose of which is to exchange the value in the display,
or X register, with that in the "working," or Y register. It

is necessary to have the registers in proper juxtaposition before pressing the $\boxed{P \rightarrow R}$ function so that the calculator can perform the polar-rectangular conversion correctly. Check this positioning requirement on your own instrument. Some models operate in reverse fashion to the TI-55. You will notice that courses have been entered as three-figure numbers for consistency, although the calculator accepts 75, say, exactly the same way it does 075.

Returning to our practical example, the actual key-punch program to solve it would proceed as follows:

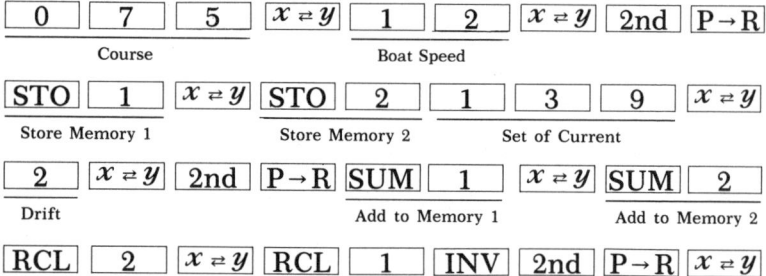

You will see that this program produces two answers. The course made good, 083°, is displayed at the next-to-last keystroke after the rectangular mode is reconverted to polar, and the speed made good, 13 knots, after the last key is pressed, reversing the X and Y registers. Should the course appearing in the display be a negative number, simply add 360° to arrive at the correct course.

A variation of this program is the determination of the current's direction and velocity from the vessel's course and speed through the water and the course and speed it actually makes good. In this case, the rectangular components of the first known vector are *subtracted* from those of the second to derive the resultant vector—the set and drift of the current.

As an example, if you steered a course of 075° at speed 12 knots but actually made good 13 knots on course 083°, what would the set and drift of the current be? The calculator program would look like this:

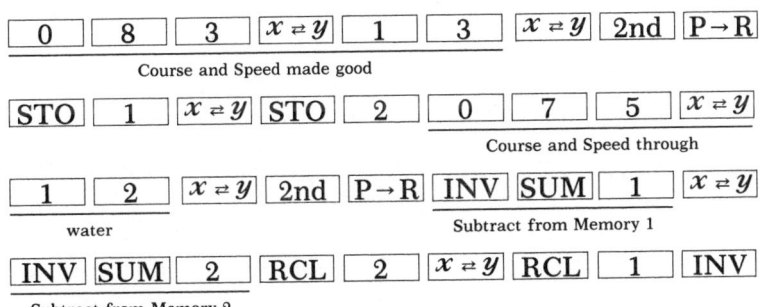

| 0 | 8 | 3 | $x \rightleftarrows y$ | 1 | 3 | $x \rightleftarrows y$ | 2nd | P→R |

Course and Speed made good

| STO | 1 | $x \rightleftarrows y$ | STO | 2 | 0 | 7 | 5 | $x \rightleftarrows y$ |

Course and Speed through

| 1 | 2 | $x \rightleftarrows y$ | 2nd | P→R | INV | SUM | 1 | $x \rightleftarrows y$ |

water   Subtract from Memory 1

| INV | SUM | 2 | RCL | 2 | $x \rightleftarrows y$ | RCL | 1 | INV |

Subtract from Memory 2

2nd P→R $x \rightleftarrows y$ Following the procedure in the previous problem, the direction of the set, 139°, is displayed after the next-to-last keypunch, and the drift rate, 2 knots, after the registers have been exchanged.

It is also possible to determine set and drift from the difference between a fix and the corresponding Dead Reckoning position. This will be discussed in connection with Program P.7. In small boats, however, the characteristics of the current are most often determined by tables, current charts, or simply by observation.

V.2 Current Sailing—Course and Speed Required

Another version of the current sailing problem occurs when the course and speed to be made good are known, together with the current's set and drift, and the navigator wants to determine the course and speed required to make good his objectives. In this case, the rectangular components of the current vector are subtracted from those of the vector representing the intended track, resulting in the course to steer and the speed required.

Follow this practical example: The course and speed to be made good are 083° at 13 knots. The current is flowing toward 139° at 2 knots. What course and speed are required to make good the intended track? The calculator sequence would be:

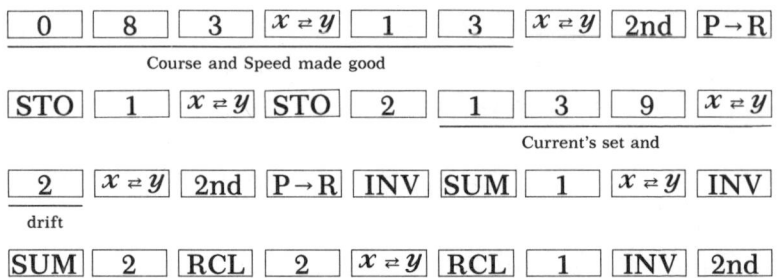

$\boxed{P \to R}\;\boxed{x \rightleftarrows y}$ As in the preceding examples, the course the vessel is required to steer, 075°, is displayed after the reconversion from rectangular to polar, and the speed required, 12 knots, after the final register exchange. Again, 360° should be added if the course displayed is negative.

The third case in current sailing—that in which the course to steer and the actual speed made good are found from the course to be made good, the vessel's speed through the water, and the set and drift—requires a somewhat different solution involving trigonometric functions. This will be discussed in Program P.1 in Chapter 5.

V.3 Direction and Velocity of True Wind

Vector arithmetic is also the process used for solving true/apparent wind problems. Knowing the vessel's course and speed, and the direction and velocity of the apparent wind, the navigator can readily determine the true wind direction and speed by subtracting the N–S and E–W components of the vessel's track vector from those of the apparent wind.

If, for example, a ship on course 045° at 10 knots records an apparent wind of 18 knots from the north (000°), what is the velocity and direction of the true wind? The vector arithmetic is performed on the calculator as follows:

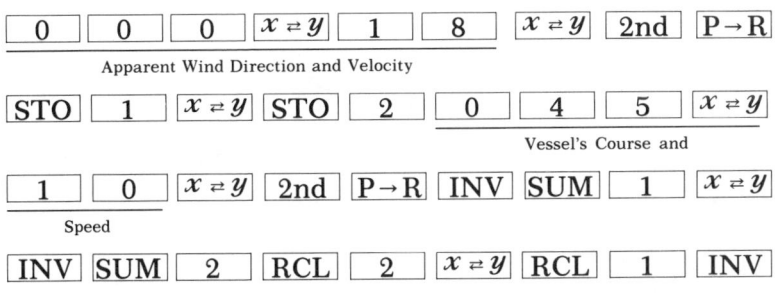

Apparent Wind Direction and Velocity

Vessel's Course and

Speed

$\boxed{\text{2nd}}$ $\boxed{\text{P}\to\text{R}}$ $\boxed{x \rightleftarrows y}$ You will see displayed after the next-to-last step a negative value requiring the addition of 360° to yield the true wind direction, 327°. The true wind velocity, 13 knots, appears after the final step in the sequence.

Should you wish to perform this exercise in reverse, you would simply *add* the vessel's vector components to those of the *true* wind to obtain the direction and velocity of the *apparent* wind.

V.4 Traverse Sailing

Traverse sailing is a method of determining the single course and distance equivalent to a series of courses and distances actually sailed. Since the solution is based on the assumption that the surface is a plane, it loses its practical accuracy with distances of more than a few hundred miles. As an example, illustrated in Figure 4-3, the navigator's log of a particular voyage reads, "From Point *A*, steered course 116° for 1 mile; changed course to 084° for 0.5 miles; changed course to 013° for 1 mile, arriving at Point *D*." What is the equivalent course and distance directly from *A* to *D*?

The calculator solution, just like the preceding examples in current sailing, involves changing each leg to its rectangular components and, after finding their algebraic sums, changing back to the polar mode to express the equivalent, direct course and distance. The keypunch program, which you will find quite similar to those that have gone before, is as follows:

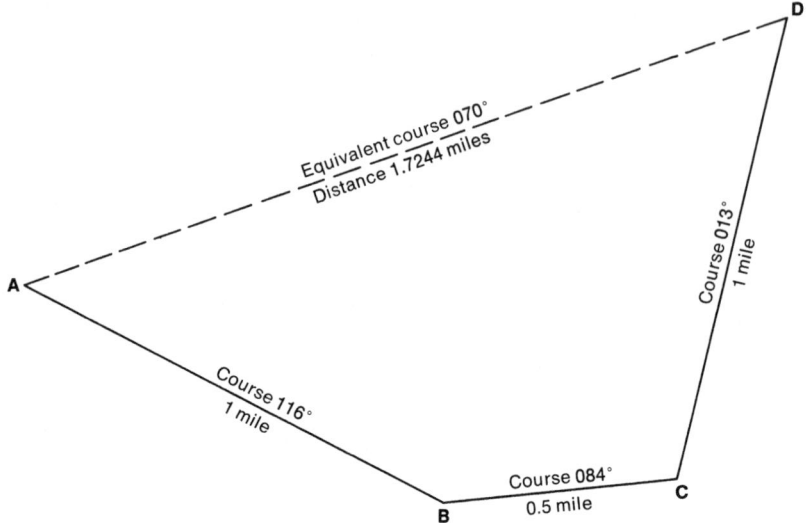

Figure 4-3. The geometry of a traverse.

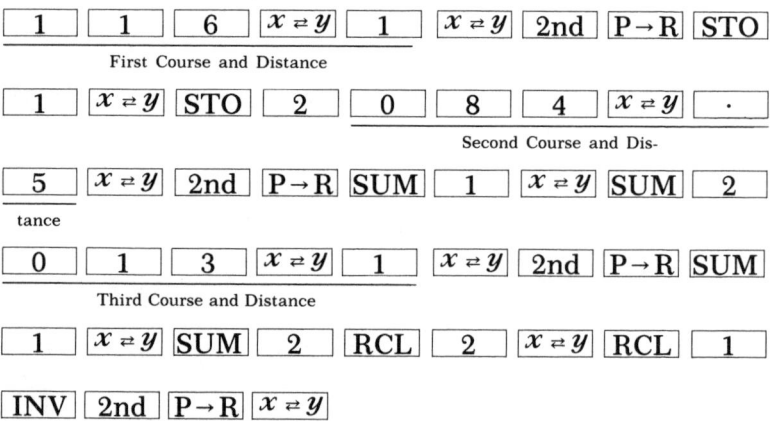

As in the previous examples, the display after the reconversion from rectangular to polar represents the direct course, 070°, while the final display, after reversing the registers, indicates the equivalent direct distance between points *A* and *D,* 1.7244 miles. In any case in which the course display is a negative value, add 360° to obtain the proper figure.

V.5 Bearing and Distance to Destination

An alternate use of a traverse is the determination of the course and distance remaining to a mark, or other destination, having known the direct course and distance from the starting point and the respective values of each of the intermediate legs.

Referring again to Figure 4-3, if it was known that the course and distance from Starting Point *A* to Destination *D* was 070° and 1.7244 miles, the navigator could determine after sailing the first two legs (116° for 1 mile, and 084° for 0.5 miles) that the bearing and distance remaining to Destination *D* from his location *C* was 013° and 1 mile by using a calculator program like this:

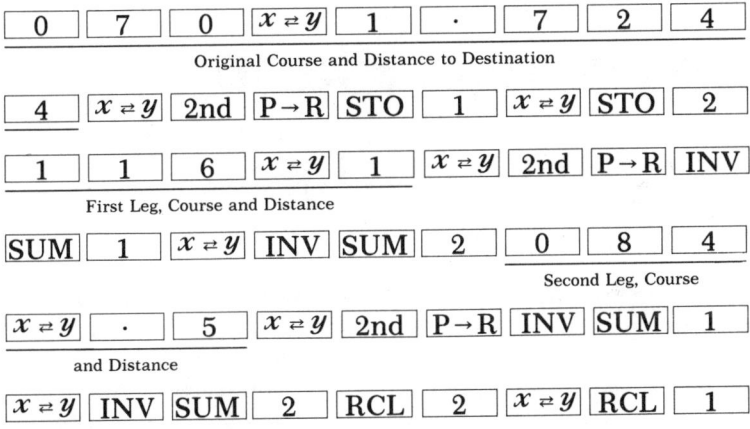

Original Course and Distance to Destination

First Leg, Course and Distance

Second Leg, Course

and Distance

INV 2nd P→R $x \rightleftharpoons y$ The bearing is displayed after the next-to-last step and the remaining distance after the last. The 360° rule also applies if the bearing display is negative. You will notice a repetitive pattern in all the vector arithmetic exercises. It is a worthwhile pattern to master as the technique is widely applicable in the solution of navigation problems.

5. Solutions Involving Plane Trigonometry

The mathematical procedures of plane trigonometry and the natural trig functions—sine, cosine, tangent, and their inverses—are used in solving a number of navigation problems, usually dealing with the properties of triangles. As in the case of Traverse Sailing, Program V.4, the assumption is made that the triangle lies in a plane. Since the earth's surface is spherical, however, the practical accuracy of the plane solution decreases as the dimensions exceed a few hundred miles. As a consequence, for very long distances, such as those involved in celestial navigation, the somewhat more complicated spherical trigonometry procedures may be required. These are discussed in Chapter 6.

P.1 Current Sailing—Course to Steer; Speed Made Good

One case in current sailing most expeditiously solved by the use of trig functions is that in which the navigator knows the course he wants to make good and the vessel's available speed through the water in addition to his estimate of the current's set and drift. What he wishes to calculate is the course he should steer and the resulting speed made good over his intended track. Assume, for example, that a navigator wishes to make good a course of 083° through a current setting toward 139° at 2 knots, while his boatspeed will be 12 knots. What course should he steer, and what speed will actually be made good over his intended track of 083°? Try this program, which, as you can see, is shortened by taking advantage of five memory registers. It could be solved with fewer memories, however, by recording and reentering the intermediate data as it is called for.

1	2	STO	1	0	8	3	STO	2

Boat Speed   Course to Make Good

+/−	+	1	3	9	=	STO	3	sin

Set of Current

STO	4	×	2	÷	RCL	1	=	INV

Drift

sin	STO	5	+	RCL	3	=	+/−	+

1	8	0	=	sin	×	RCL	1	÷

RCL   4   =   The answer, 13 knots, represents the speed made good along the intended track, 083°. The program continues: RCL   5   +/−   +   RCL   2   = , and the final display, 075°, is the course to steer. Should that display be negative, 360° is added to yield the proper course. Your answers can be double-checked by testing through the first current sailing program, V.1, entering that program with the steering course, the vessel's speed, and the set and drift of the current. The answers should coincide with the intended track and the speed made good along it.

Some navigators prefer to solve this current problem for the "course correction angle"—the amount to *change* course to arrive at the proper course to steer. This can be done in three steps:

• Estimate the current's velocity and divide it into the vessel's speed to obtain the ratio:

$$\frac{\text{Vessel Speed}}{\text{Current Velocity}}$$

which we'll call "Current Ratio."

• Estimate the relative angle of the current's set to the ship's heading, which we'll call "Current Angle."

• Apply the formula:

$$\text{Sin}-1\left(\frac{\text{Sin Current Angle}}{\text{Current Ratio}}\right)$$

to obtain the "Course Correction Angle" to be applied to the intended track to determine the course to steer.

When this procedure is completed, by then applying the formula:

$$\frac{\text{Sin }(180°-\text{Course Correction Angle}-\text{Current Angle})}{\text{Sin Current Angle}}$$

a "speed factor" is derived, which, when multiplied by the vessel's speed, yields the speed made good.

Returning to the practical example in the first part of this program, the calculator sequence would proceed as follows:

| 1 2 | ÷ | 2 | = | displays the "Cur-

Vessel Speed   Current Velocity

rent Ratio," 6.

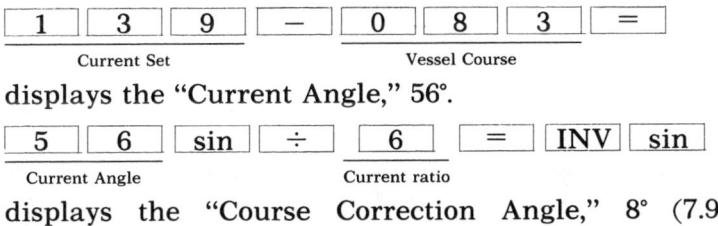

displays the "Current Angle," 56°.

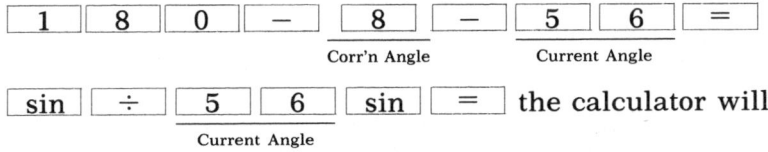

displays the "Course Correction Angle," 8° (7.942), which, applied to the track of 083°, yields the course to steer, 075°.

Next, by keying:

| 1 | 8 | 0 | − | 8 | − | 5 | 6 | = |

Corr'n Angle   Current Angle

| sin | ÷ | 5 | 6 | sin | = | the calculator will

Current Angle

compute and display the "speed factor," 1.08, which, multiplied by the vessel's speed of 12 knots, produces the speed, 13 knots, made good over the intended track.

The virtue of this solution is that it requires somewhat fewer keypunches and may be slightly easier to follow at the outset, although I prefer the first method, since it eliminates any ambiguity as to the direction in which the course correction angle should be applied.

P.2 Sailing Tactics—Extra Distance Traveled

An interesting challenge facing the sailing yachtsman is the decision as to how far he can afford to deviate from the course he is sailing to gain extra speed. Both on the wind, where bearing off will add to boatspeed, and tacking downwind, to take advantage of the fact that most sailboats reach faster than they run, the navigator must make a compromise between the extra speed gained and the extra distance traveled.

The formula which applies is:

$$\text{Distance Ratio} = \frac{1}{\text{Cosine, Angle of Deviation}}$$

Thus, if a vessel on a downwind leg alters course 20° to increase boatspeed, the calculator program ⎡ 1 ⎤ ⎡ ÷ ⎤ ⎡ 2 ⎤ ⎡ 0 ⎤ ⎡ cos ⎤ ⎡ = ⎤ indicates that the distance traveled will be 1.06 times, or just 6 percent more than the distance by the direct course. Accordingly, if the speed resulting from the course alteration is more than 1.06 times the former speed, the navigator will have profitably shortened his time to the mark.

Tacking upwind, a sailboat may already be deviating from the direct course to a windward mark by 45 degrees, which, by calculation, represents a ratio of 1.41, or 41 percent extra distance to be sailed. Bearing off another 10 degrees (then 55 degrees off the direct line) produces a distance ratio of 1.74, or 33 percent *additional* distance to be traveled. Thus, the calculator program shows that the boatspeed must be increased by more than one-third, under these circumstances, to make the tactic of bearing off beneficial.

P.3 Distance-off by Vertical Angle

The sextant, primarily used for measuring altitudes in celestial navigation, may also be used to measure the angle between the lines of sight to the top of an object of known height and to its base or, if its base is beyond the visible horizon, to the visible horizon.

The vertical angle measured by the sextant must, in each instance, be corrected for index error (see Program A.7, Sextant Corrections), and in the latter case, where the base is beyond the horizon, also for the height of eye—the Dip Correction. The approximate distance-off, normally expressed in nautical miles, can be determined by calculator following the programs illustrated in each of the following examples:

(a) A tower 92 feet high, whose waterline can be seen, is

subtended by a vertical Sextant Angle, corrected for index error, of 0°15.0′. What is the distance-off? The keypunch sequence is:

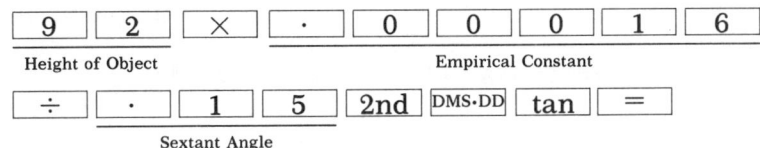

The last display indicates the distance, 3.37 nautical miles.

(b) The same 92-foot tower, with its base beyond the horizon, is observed from a height of eye of 12 feet. The Sextant Angle, measured from the top of the tower to the horizon, and corrected for index error and Dip, is 0°07.0′. What is the distance-off? The program in this case follows these steps:

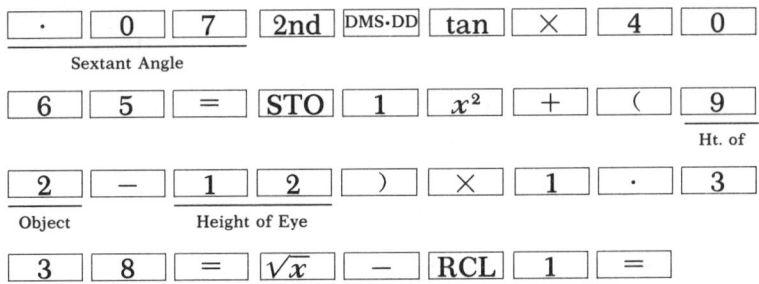

The answer displayed, 4.97, is the distance-off in nautical miles.

Note the use of the word approximate in first describing the distance-off solutions. This is because atmospheric aberrations, and a moving deck, can make exact low-altitude readings difficult to obtain on the sextant, and the constants used, which have been arrived at empirically, are approximations in themselves.

P.4 Distance-off by Two Bearings

Distance-off problems involving the measurement of horizontal angles, solved conventionally by plotting or by *Bowditch* tables, lend themselves to calculator solutions based on the properties of right and oblique plane triangles. One typical example is illustrated in Figure 5-1.

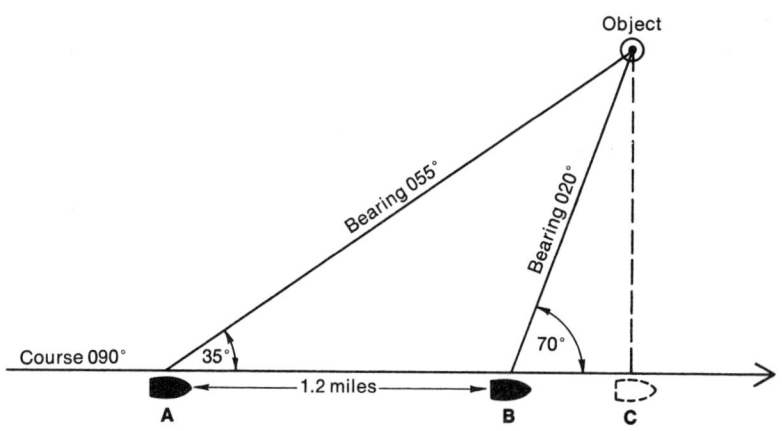

Figure 5-1. Distance-off by two bearings, same object.

In this example, a navigator on course 090° takes a bearing of an object from Point *A* (reading 055°) and, having run 1.2 miles to Point *B,* takes another bearing of the same object (this time reading 020°). How far will the navigator be from the object at the time of the second bearing, at Point *B,* and how far off will he be when the object is abeam, at Point *C*? The answers can be obtained by keystroking as follows:

0	9	0	STO	1	−	0	5	5

Course   First Bearing

=	STO	2	sin	STO	3	1	8	0

+	0	2	0	−	RCL	1	=	STO

Second Bearing

1	+	RCL	2	=	+/−	+	1	8

0	=	sin	STO	2	1	·	2	÷

Distance Travelled

RCL	2	=	STO	2	×	RCL	3	=

The answer displayed, 1.2 miles, is the distance-off at the second bearing. Sharp-eyed navigators will recognize this as the classic case of "doubling the angle on the bow" and can confirm that the answer is correct. To find the distance-off when the object is abeam, the program continues

RCL	2	×	RCL	1	sin	=	×	RCL

3	=

. The final display, 1.1276 miles, is the distance off the observed object at the time it is abeam.

P.5 Height of Tide at any Time

The determination of the height of the tide at any time is an exercise requiring natural trig functions in addition to sexagesimal/decimal conversions and the four arithmetic functions. It is a good test of your facility in combining a number of the calculator features to which you have been introduced so far.

A common problem for navigators traversing tidal waters in which the ship's draft is critical, the tide level is based on the assumption that the relationship between time and the height of the tide takes the form of a sine curve. Given the predicted times and heights of the nearest high and low waters from the *Tide Tables,* the solution can be found by calculator, by graphic diagram (such as given in *Bowditch,* Vol. I, 1977, Art. 1206), or by using Table 3 in the *Tide Tables*—the latter two methods being approximate.

In the calculator solution, the input data can be entered when called for in the program or, if the instrument has sufficient memory registers (five is ideal), it is much easier to enter all the information at the outset. That is what has been done in the following sequence.

- Enter the time of the nearest *low* water (in the usual form: hours, *decimal point*, minutes), convert it to decimal hours by pressing ⌷2nd⌷ ⌷DMS·DD⌷, and store the result in memory register 1, ⌷STO⌷ ⌷ 1 ⌷.

- Enter the time of the nearest *high* water, press ⌷2nd⌷ ⌷DMS·DD⌷ ⌷STO⌷ ⌷ 2 ⌷.

- Enter the height of *low* water (in feet, from the *Tide Tables*), press ⌷+/−⌷ if negative, ⌷STO⌷ ⌷ 3 ⌷.

- Enter the height of *high* water, ⌷STO⌷ ⌷ 4 ⌷.

When you are ready to run the program, enter the time at which the height is to be determined, press ⌷2nd⌷ ⌷DMS·DD⌷ ⌷STO⌷ ⌷ 5 ⌷ and proceed with the following keystroke sequence:

⌷RCL⌷ ⌷ 4 ⌷ ⌷ − ⌷ ⌷RCL⌷ ⌷ 3 ⌷ ⌷ = ⌷ ⌷STO⌷ ⌷ 4 ⌷ ⌷RCL⌷

⌷ 5 ⌷ ⌷ − ⌷ ⌷RCL⌷ ⌷ 1 ⌷ ⌷ = ⌷ ⌷ ÷ ⌷ ⌷ (⌷ ⌷RCL⌷ ⌷ 2 ⌷

⌷ − ⌷ ⌷RCL⌷ ⌷ 1 ⌷ ⌷) ⌷ ⌷ = ⌷ ⌷STO⌷ ⌷ 2 ⌷ ⌷ − ⌷ ⌷ · ⌷

⌷ 1 ⌷ ⌷ 0 ⌷ ⌷ 5 ⌷ ⌷ × ⌷ ⌷ (⌷ ⌷ 3 ⌷ ⌷ 6 ⌷ ⌷ 0 ⌷ ⌷ × ⌷

$\boxed{\text{RCL}}$ $\boxed{\quad 2 \quad}$ $\boxed{\quad) \quad}$ $\boxed{\sin}$ $\boxed{\quad = \quad}$ $\boxed{\times}$ $\boxed{\text{RCL}}$ $\boxed{\quad 4 \quad}$ $\boxed{\quad = \quad}$

$\boxed{\quad + \quad}$ $\boxed{\text{RCL}}$ $\boxed{\quad 3 \quad}$ $\boxed{\quad = \quad}$ The final display will show the height of the tide in feet above the chart datum at the selected time.

Let's try a practical example. On March 27, 1975, Low Water at The Battery in New York occurred at 1416, with the following High Water at 2025. The heights were -1.2 and $+5.7$ feet, respectively, from the chart sounding datum. What would the height have been at 1620? The answer, which you can confirm by Table 3 of the *Tide Tables,* or, if you prefer, by tide graph, should be 0.5 feet above datum (which represents a 1.7-foot rise over the Low Water height of -1.2 feet).

P.6 Dead Reckoning Position

The object of this program is to obtain the latitude and longitude of the Dead Reckoning position by applying the course and distance sailed to the latitude and longitude of the point of departure. The procedure is to convert the course-distance vector to its rectangular components, change those to their latitude and longitude equivalents, and add them algebraically to the respective coordinates of the initial position.

In the case of the latitude, the computation is straight-forward, adopting the convention that one nautical mile is equivalent to one minute of latitude anywhere on earth. Longitude, on the other hand, is a different matter, since the length of a minute of longitude becomes progressively less with increasing latitude, as the meridians converge at the poles. "Mid-latitude sailing," which is used in this program, utilizes the relationship between the E–W distance and the units of longitude as it exists at the *middle* latitude between the departure point and the final position. The correct difference in longitude, so obtained, is the one applied to the initial longitude to produce the longitudinal coordinate of the Dead Reckoning position.

For navigators interested in the mathematics, the formula used in mid-latitude sailing is: Difference in longitude equals "departure" times the secant ($\frac{1}{\text{cosine}}$) of the middle latitude, where "departure" equals distance times the sine of the course (in other words, "departure" is the E–W component of the course-distance vector).

The calculator program can be illustrated by a practical example. Starting from a point at Latitude 26°45.0′N, Longitude 60°15.0′W, a vessel sails 98 miles on course 135°. What will its position be then?

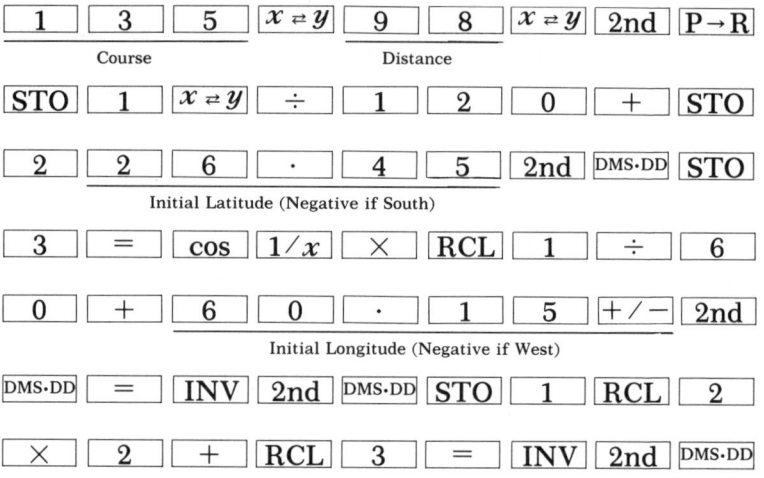

The last display represents the Dead Reckoning Latitude, 25°35.7′N. To produce the DR Longitude, press RCL 1 and display that answer, 58°57.8′W. Note that it is *West* because the value displayed was negative.

If several courses and speeds are sailed between the point of origin and the DR position, after the third register exchange, $x \rightleftarrows y$, (keypunch number twelve), store the contents of the display in memory register 2 by pressing STO 2. Then, following the procedure of Program V.4, Traverse Sailing, convert each subsequent leg into its rectangular components and add them to the respective memories, using the SUM key. When all the legs have been accumulated, recall the contents of memory register 2 by pressing RCL 2 and, starting with the division sign ⎡ ÷ ⎤ (keypunch number thirteen in the original program), follow the sequence to its conclusion.

You will find this program works without error when proceeding either way across the equator as long as you observe the convention that North latitudes are displayed positively and South latitudes with a negative sign. Proceeding easterly across the International Date Line (180° E or W), 360° should be subtracted from East longitudes (rendering the equivalent West longitude) to produce a correct result. Proceeding westbound, the answer displayed will be in terms of West longitude, and it should be added algebraically to 360° to produce the correct East longitude.

P.7 Rhumb-line Navigation—Course & Distance

The reverse of the previous program, P.6, is the determination of the course and distance between two points whose geographic coordinates are known, using mid-latitude sailing.

If, for example, a navigator fixes his position at Latitude 25°35.7′N, Longitude 58°57.8′W, having departed from Latitude 26°45.0′N, Longitude 60°15.0′W, what is the course and distance sailed between those two points? The keystroke sequence would be:

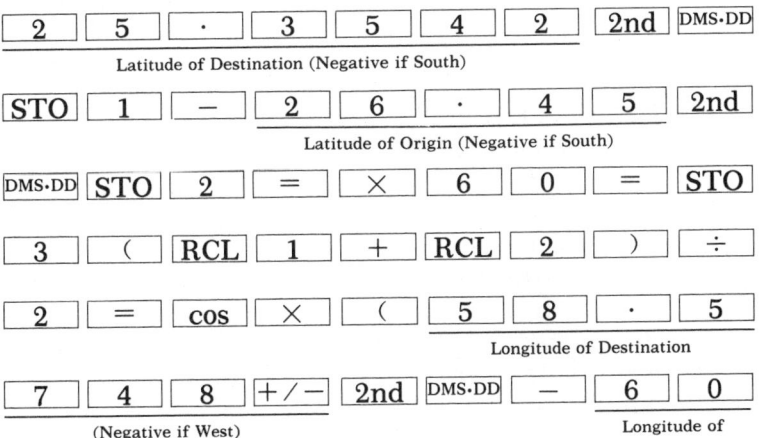

| 2 | 5 | · | 3 | 5 | 4 | 2 | 2nd | DMS·DD |

Latitude of Destination (Negative if South)

| STO | 1 | — | 2 | 6 | · | 4 | 5 | 2nd |

Latitude of Origin (Negative if South)

| DMS·DD | STO | 2 | = | × | 6 | 0 | = | STO |

| 3 | (| RCL | 1 | + | RCL | 2 |) | ÷ |

| 2 | = | cos | × | (| 5 | 8 | · | 5 |

Longitude of Destination

| 7 | 4 | 8 | +/− | 2nd | DMS·DD | — | 6 | 0 |

(Negative if West)   Longitude of

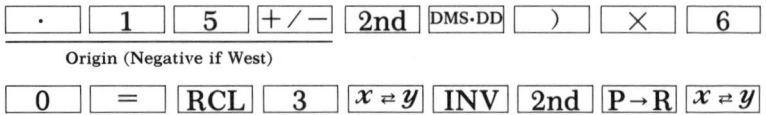

Origin (Negative if West)

As in the vector arithmetic programs, the course, 135°, is displayed at the next-to-last step after returning to the polar mode and the distance, 98 miles, after the registers are reversed. Should a course shown be negative, add 360° to display the correct course. If the two positions straddle the International Date Line, East longitudes should be entered as East longitude *minus* 360°.

This program also provides a means of determining the current's set and drift. By using a fix as the destination and the corresponding DR position as the point of origin, the resulting course will represent the set, while the distance found, divided by the hours elapsed since the previous fix, will indicate the current's drift in knots.

6. Solutions Involving Spherical Trigonometry

The very mention of spherical trig is enough to frighten most mortals, even though it only extends the concepts of plane trigonometry to the properties of triangles on a spherical surface. It is the highest branch of mathematics normally used by the navigator, and lends itself to the solution of a variety of problems in celestial navigation as well as those dealing with the curved surface of the globe where large distances are involved.

S.1 Great-Circle Sailing—Course and Distance

The shortest distance between two points on the surface of a sphere is a great-circle—the curve formed by the intersection of the surface with a plane on which the two points are located, passing through the center of the sphere. Meridians of longitude are examples of great-circles on earth.

A navigator planning a long sea voyage may elect to follow the great-circle route rather than the longer rhumb line, even though the latter *appears* as a straight line on the usual nautical (Mercator) chart. Since the great-circle track is constantly changing direction as the vessel proceeds and would appear as a curve on a Mercator chart, it is common practice to calculate the distance and initial course, which this program does, the vertex, found in Program S.2, and a series of intermediate points along the track. These intermediate points are then plotted on the chart, connected by straight lines, and provide the succession of rhumb-line courses the vessel actually sails. The process is called "Composite Sailing" and, if the legs are reasonably short, particularly in the higher latitudes, the resulting track will closely approximate the great-circle.

Great-circle tracks can also be found by plotting on a special (gnomonic) great-circle chart. The track appears as a straight line connecting the departure and destination. Intermediate points may be taken off at the intersection of the track with selected longitudes. The ease of making a gnomonic plot on a great-circle chart, and the advantage of being able to visualize the relationship of the track with the surrounding geographical features, recommends the method, although the distance and initial course are most accurately checked by the calculator solution.

This first great-circle program computes the distance between two geographical points by the great-circle (shortest) route. This can be compared with the rhumb-line distance calculated by mid-latitude sailing, Program P.7, to get an idea of the saving. This program then proceeds to determine the initial course to steer from the point of departure.

The computation itself involves the solution of an oblique spherical triangle, and any of the methods of spherical trigonometry for solving such triangles can be used. Care must always be taken to apply the rules correctly to avoid ambiguity, which may arise when the trigonometric function used does not indicate the quadrant in which the solution applies. You must also avoid the selection of points exactly opposite on the globe (antipodal) for which the solution is indeterminate. In cases where the longitude of the two points, departure and destination, are identical, the initial course will be 000° or 180° and, although the calculator solution in that circumstance is also indeterminate, it is of little import since the answer is obvious.

Because of the number of steps involved, this program, like P.5, is easier to run if the entering data are punched in and stored in the memory registers before the actual sequence begins. If sufficient memories are not available in your instrument, the information can be entered as it is called for in the program, simply slowing down your execution time. Latitudes and longitudes, consistent with our preselected convention, are punched in, their signs changed to negative (pressing $\boxed{+/-}$) in case of South latitudes or West longitudes, and converted to degrees and decimals by pressing $\boxed{\text{2nd}}$ $\boxed{\text{DMS·DD}}$. With these comments in mind, let's look at a practical problem.

A vessel departs from Chesapeake Bay Entrance, Latitude 36°57.7′N, Longitude 75°42.2′W, bound for Bordeaux, France, Latitude 45°39.1′N, Longitude 1°29.8′W. What is the distance and the initial course on the great-circle track?

The variable inputs are loaded into the memories as follows:

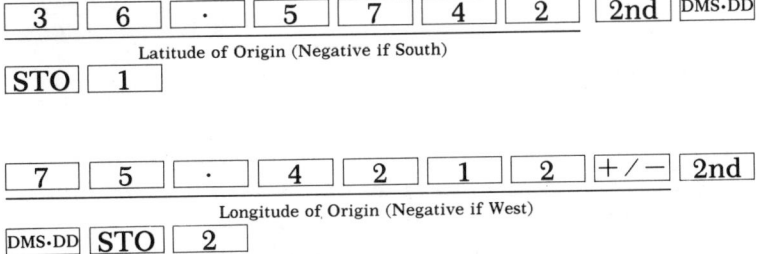

$\boxed{3}$ $\boxed{6}$ $\boxed{\cdot}$ $\boxed{5}$ $\boxed{7}$ $\boxed{4}$ $\boxed{2}$ $\boxed{\text{2nd}}$ $\boxed{\text{DMS·DD}}$
Latitude of Origin (Negative if South)
$\boxed{\text{STO}}$ $\boxed{1}$

$\boxed{7}$ $\boxed{5}$ $\boxed{\cdot}$ $\boxed{4}$ $\boxed{2}$ $\boxed{1}$ $\boxed{2}$ $\boxed{+/-}$ $\boxed{\text{2nd}}$
Longitude of Origin (Negative if West)
$\boxed{\text{DMS·DD}}$ $\boxed{\text{STO}}$ $\boxed{2}$

| 4 | 5 | . | 3 | 9 | 0 | 6 | 2nd | DMS·DD |

Latitude of Destination (Negative if South)

| STO | 3 |

| 1 | . | 2 | 9 | 4 | 8 | +/− | 2nd | DMS·DD |

Longitude of Destination (Negative if West)

| STO | 4 |

Then the program is run:

| RCL | 2 | − | RCL | 4 | = | STO | 4 | cos |

| × | RCL | 3 | cos | × | RCL | 1 | cos | = |

| + | RCL | 1 | sin | × | RCL | 3 | sin | = |

| INV | cos | STO | 5 | × | 6 | 0 | = |

The answer displayed is the distance, 3264.5 nautical miles, along the great-circle route. The distance in degrees of arc and the difference in the longitudes have been stored, in the course of the program, in memory registers 5 and 4, respectively, so the next stage—the determination of initial course—continues without having to reenter these values.

| RCL | 1 | cos | × | RCL | 5 | sin | = | 1/x |

| × | (| RCL | 1 | sin | × | RCL | 5 | cos |

| +/− | + | RCL | 3 | sin |) | = | INV | cos |

Rules must now be applied to the "course angle," *C,* which is displayed at the end of the program, to find the correct course, Cn, to steer. With the calculator still on, press RCL 4 sin , and if the value displayed is negative, Cn equals *C.* If, on the other hand, the sine of the contents of memory 4 is positive, Cn = 360°−*C.* Common sense will usually tell you if your answer is logical, even without your having to apply the test.

In our practical example, the answer displayed, 55.8069, or 55.8°, is the "course angle," and since the sine of the longitude difference in memory 4 is negative, the initial course to steer, Cn, is the same.

If you are going to proceed with Program S.2, the longitude of the destination should be restored to memory 4 and the correct initial course, Cn, entered into memory register 5. In this way, the input data will all be in the machine's memories preparatory to starting the next sequence. If you are able to utilize more than five memories on your calculator—as you can on the TI-55—you can store the difference in longitude at the eighth program step in register 6, and the correct initial course in register 7, substituting those register numbers in the appropriate places in Program S.2, thereby eliminating the reentry step.

For those readers interested in the mathematical aspects of the great-circle solution, there is a comprehensive treatise in *Bowditch*. From that source the formula for determining distance has been derived:

$$60 \cos^{-1}(\sin L_1 \sin L_2 + \cos L_1 \cos L_2 \cos DLo)$$

and, for finding "course angle," *C:*

$$\cos^{-1}\left(\frac{\sin L_2 - \sin L_1 \cos D°}{\cos L_1 \sin D°}\right)$$

S.2 Great-Circle Sailing—Vertex and Points Along Track

If it is desired to locate the vertex (the point of maximum latitude) and intermediate points along a great-circle route by computation, the following program may be used. To demonstrate, the same departure and destination as used in S.1 will apply (L_1 36°57.7'N, λ_1 75°42.2'W; L_2 45° 39.1'N, λ_2 1°29.8'W), with initial course 055.8° (55.8069 is in the calculator in memory 5 if carried forward from S.1).

If the calculator is not already loaded with all the input data, as would be the case if Program S.1 was followed to its conclusion and the instrument left on, it should be reloaded as follows:

Latitude of origin in degrees and decimals (negative if South) in memory 1;

Longitude of origin in degrees and decimals (negative if West) in memory 2;

Latitude of destination in degrees and decimals (negative if South) in memory 3;

Longitude of destination in degrees and decimals (negative if West) in memory 4;

Course, Cn, in degrees and decimals in memory 5.

The keystroke sequence, which first finds the longitude of the vertex, proceeds like this:

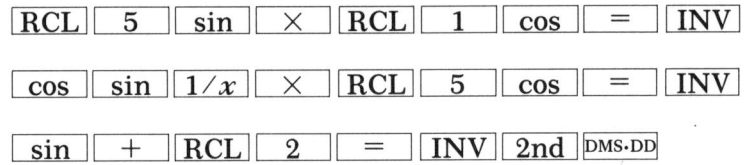

In this example, the longitude of the vertex is 27°12.7′ W. Had the value in the display exceeded 180° it would have been necessary to apply 360° with the proper sign to identify the correct hemisphere.

To find the latitude corresponding to any longitude along the great-circle track (including the latitude of the vertex whose longitude you have just determined), the selected longitude is keyed in, changed to degrees and decimals, marked with a negative sign if West, and stored in Memory 5. The keypunch sequence then proceeds:

| RCL | 3 | tan | × | (| RCL | 5 | − | RCL |

| 2 |) | sin | − | RCL | 1 | tan | × | (|

| RCL | 5 | − | RCL | 4 |) | sin | = | ÷ |

| (| RCL | 4 | − | RCL | 2 |) | sin | = |

INV tan INV 2nd DMS·DD displaying the latitude sought (in the case of the vertex in our example, 48°37.8′ N). By leaving the calculator on, as many different points as desired can be determined by entering the selected longitude and solving for the corresponding latitude. In this exercise, for example, the latitude of the intersection of the great-circle track with the meridian of 60°W is 43°40.1′ N; with 40°W, 47°54.9′N; and with 20°W, 48°24.2′N.

The longitude corresponding to any selected latitude along the great-circle route can also be found, and this may be useful if, for example, the navigator does not wish to exceed a certain maximum latitude and wants to know the first point at which the track will intersect it. Naturally, the latitude selected must be within the limits of the points of origin and destination and the vertex—greater latitudes will simply produce an indeterminate solution.

Noting that L_x represents the selected latitude, with a negative sign if South; L_v the latitude of the vertex found in the earlier part of the program, also negative if South; and λ_v the longitude of the vertex, negative if West, the calculator sequence goes as follows:

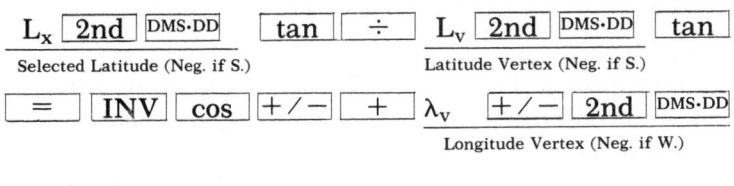

L_x 2nd DMS·DD   tan   ÷ L_v 2nd DMS·DD   tan
Selected Latitude (Neg. if S.)   Latitude Vertex (Neg. if S.)

=   INV   cos   +/−   + λ_v +/−   2nd   DMS·DD
                                Longitude Vertex (Neg. if W.)

=   INV   2nd   DMS·DD

As before, if the display is greater than 180°, subtract 360° if it is positive, or add 360° if the sign is negative, thereby yielding the correct longitude corresponding to the selected latitude. In our example, latitude 42°N is crossed by the great-circle track at 64°44.8′W; and latitude 47°N at longitude 46°24.2′W.

To the nonmathematicians who may have found this exercise a little more that they had bargained for, take heart. Not only is this the most difficult program in the text, and one that many navigators would never even undertake until calculators came on the scene, but, as pointed out earlier, its principal elements can be determined graphically and, with a gnomonic chart at hand, most navigators prefer that solution.

S.3 Sight Reduction

The area in which hand-held calculators of the scientific variety have probably made their greatest impact on the practice of navigation is in the solution of celestial observations—the process called "sight reduction." The computation, as in the case of the great-circle problems, is based on the trigonometric solution of a spherical triangle, the "navigational triangle."

A great number of methods for accomplishing this solution have been advanced over the years. *Bowditch* devotes an entire chapter of some fifty-seven pages to a comparison of the various techniques, and virtually any of the formulae can be worked on a modern calculator. For a manual calculator, however, a sequence requiring the minimum number of keystrokes is most desirable, and to this end the method described in *Bowditch,* Vol. I, 1977, Art. 2111, produces such formulae.

It is assumed that you are already familiar with the sight reduction procedure that is discussed in detail in *The Yachtsman's Guide to Celestial Navigation,* and that with the *Nautical Almanac* and our earlier programs (notably A.7, Sextant Corrections, and A.4, Sexagesimal Arithmetic) you will have been able to arrive at the point where the inspection tables, such as Pub. No. 249, begin. That is, you will have established the Local Hour Angle (LHA), the declination (Dec), and the latitude (L), and are ready to proceed with the reduction. You will, of course, be solving for the same Computed Altitude (Hc), which will be compared with your Observed Altitude (Ho) to obtain the intercept (a) and the azimuth angle (Z), which, when adjusted for the proper quadrant, produces the true azimuth (Zn), providing all the information needed to complete the plotting of the line of position.

An attractive feature of the calculator solution is that your DR latitude and longitude can be used instead of an assumed position, since neither LHA nor latitude have to be entered in whole degrees the way they do in the inspection tables. This has the great advantage of your being able to plot the intercept from the DR position on the chart, and, if a line of position has to be advanced (or retired) for a running fix, its intercept and azimuth can simply be replotted from the new DR. At the same time, by knowing the coordinates of the Dead Reckoning position at the time of the second sight, the two lines of position can be utilized to arrive at the coordinates of a running fix by calculation (see Program S.4, Fix from Two Sights).

The calculator procedure for a sight reduction begins with loading the variable information into the memory registers.

- Key in the Local Hour Angle, converting it to degrees and decimals if it is not in whole degrees, and store it in memory 1.
- Enter the declination, convert it to decimal degrees, and, *if* it is of *contrary* name to the latitude (but only *if,* and this is an exception to our convention), change its sign in the display to negative. Store the declination in memory 2.
- The latitude, like the LHA, is entered on the keyboard, changed to the degree-decimal form if not in whole degrees, and stored in memory 3. Here again, the usual rule of expressing South latitudes as negative values is re-

placed by the scheme for handling the declination sign and the quadrant rules at the end of the program.

You are then ready to proceed with the keystroke sequence, which is as follows:

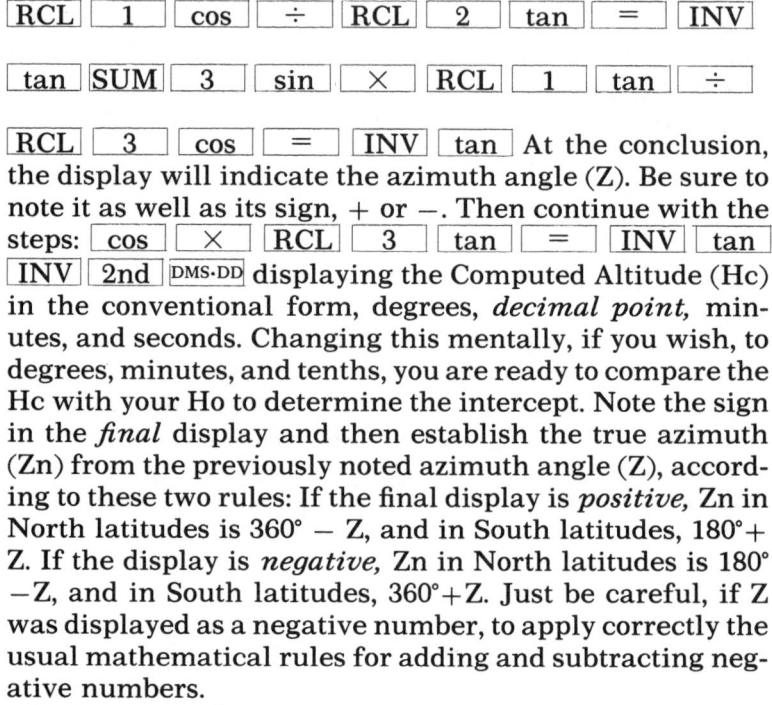

At the conclusion, the display will indicate the azimuth angle (Z). Be sure to note it as well as its sign, + or −. Then continue with the steps: cos × RCL 3 tan = INV tan INV 2nd DMS·DD displaying the Computed Altitude (Hc) in the conventional form, degrees, *decimal point,* minutes, and seconds. Changing this mentally, if you wish, to degrees, minutes, and tenths, you are ready to compare the Hc with your Ho to determine the intercept. Note the sign in the *final* display and then establish the true azimuth (Zn) from the previously noted azimuth angle (Z), according to these two rules: If the final display is *positive,* Zn in North latitudes is 360° − Z, and in South latitudes, 180°+ Z. If the display is *negative,* Zn in North latitudes is 180° −Z, and in South latitudes, 360°+Z. Just be careful, if Z was displayed as a negative number, to apply correctly the usual mathematical rules for adding and subtracting negative numbers.

Let's review this program with a practical example. A navigator in DR position, Latitude 41°00′N, Longitude 70° 27′W, observes the sun's lower limb at Sextant Altitude (hs) 66°34.8′ at 17h18m07s GMT on May 17, 1979. With data from the *Nautical Almanac,* the Sextant Altitude is corrected to the Observed Altitude (Ho) of 66°46.0′ (see Program A.7 for the calculator procedure). The daily pages and the incremental tables of the *Nautical Almanac* are entered with the time, and the sun's GHA and increment are extracted along with the sun's declination. Finally, the Local Hour Angle is calculated, by applying the DR longitude to the GHA in the usual way, and the latitude of the

DR position entered directly. This then gives you the three values, LHA (10°00′), Declination (19°18.2′, *same* name as Lat), and Latitude (41°00′), needed for either the calculator program or to enter the inspection tables. Try it both ways and see if you don't agree with the answer, Computed Altitude 66°41.0′, and Azimuth 204°.

A workbook form, slightly shortened for the calculator solution, is shown in Figure 6-1. This is quite similar to the form used in *The Yachtsman's Guide to Celestial Navigation* for the tabular reduction and you will be able to follow the exercise step by step with both methods in order to make your own comparison.

The sight reduction program can, of course, be used as a way of determining the true azimuth of the sun for checking compass error at sea. LHA, declination, and DR latitude are used in the same way as the entering arguments, and the calculator program is worked through to determine the sign (although the value isn't needed) of the final display so that the rules to obtain Zn from Z can be applied correctly. A more conventional formula for determining true azimuth is contained in Program S.7.

S.4 Fix from Two Sights

It is possible, if a navigator does not wish to plot the lines of position from his sights, to compute the coordinates of the intersection of two lines either from simultaneous observations or from sights adjusted to the same time, as in a running fix. There is a separate calculator program for the latitude and for the longitude of the fix. Each is based on the respective coordinate of the DR position (arrived at by plotting or by the Dead Reckoning Position program, P.6), and the intercepts and azimuths of the two sights.

Latitude is determined first, since it will be used in calculating the longitude difference. All our regular conventions will apply, with North latitudes and East longitudes expressed as positive values, while an intercept "toward" is positive and an intercept "away" is negative.

Date	May 17, 1979	
Body	Sun, L. L.	
hs	66 – 34. 8	
IC	– 1. 4	
D	– 2. 9	*
ha	66 – 30.5	
R	+ 15.5	*
Ho	66 – 46.0	
W	17 – 18 – 07	
corr	00	
GMT	17 – 18 – 07	
gha	75 – 55. 2	*
incr	4 – 31. 8	*
GHA	80 – 27.0	
DR λ	70 – 27. 0 W	
LHA	10	
Dec	19 – 18. 2 N	*
DR L	41 N	
Hc	66 – 41. 0	
Ho	66 – 46.0	
a	5 T	
Zn	204	

Figure 6-1. Work form for calculator sight reduction, Program S.3. Asterisked values are obtained from Nautical Almanac; *computation and solution for Hc and Z performed on calculator.*

The formula for the latitude of the fix is:

$$\text{Latitude}_{\text{Fix}} = \text{Latitude}_{\text{DR}} - \left(\frac{\text{Intercept}_2 \sin Zn_1 - \text{Intercept}_1 \sin Zn_2}{60 \sin (Zn_2 - Zn_1)}\right) .$$

The formula for finding the longitude is:

$$\text{Longitude}_{\text{Fix}} = \text{Longitude}_{\text{DR}} + \left(\frac{\text{Intercept}_2 \cos Zn_1 - \text{Intercept}_1 \cos Zn_2}{\sin (Zn_2 - Zn_1) \times 60 \cos \text{Latitude}_{\text{Fix}}}\right)$$

The calculator program is demonstrated with a practical example. From DR position, Latitude 45°20.0′N, Longitude 60°08.0′W, two simultaneous sights were taken. After reduction, the solutions were: sight one, intercept 8 miles "away," azimuth 230°; sight two, intercept 4 miles "toward," azimuth 350°. The sequence of keystrokes to determine the latitude of the fix is:

4	×	2	3	0	STO	1	sin	−
Int₂			Azimuth₁					

8	+/−	×	3	5	0	STO	2	sin
Intercept₁			Azimuth₂					

=	÷	(	RCL	2	−	RCL	1	)

sin	STO	3	÷	6	0	+/−	+	4
								DR

5	.	2	0	2nd	DMS·DD	=	STO	4
Latitude (Negative if South)								

INV 2nd DMS·DD The display, 45°25.1′N, indicates the latitude of the fix. It would have read "South" if the display had been preceded by a negative sign. In the course of the program, you will notice that the azimuths, as well as the sine of the difference in azimuths and the latitude of the fix (in degrees and decimals), have all been stored in the memory registers in preparation for continuing with the computation of the longitude of the fix, which proceeds as follows:

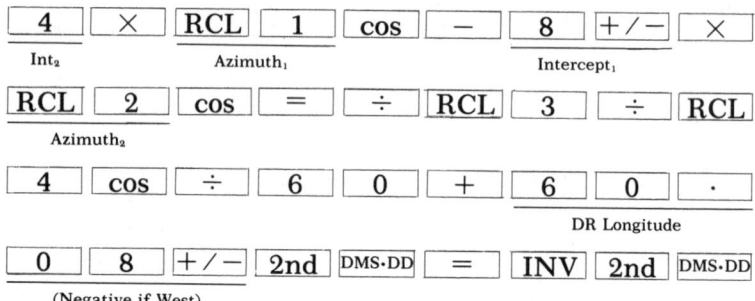

The longitude of the fix, 59°59. 3′, is displayed with a negative sign and, consequently, is West.

As discussed in Program S.3, the advantage of working from the DR position is that the two sights, even if taken at different times, can be applied to the same DR to produce, with this just-completed routine, the coordinates of a running fix. As a general rule, however, most navigators prefer to plot their lines of position, particularly if the lines intersect at small angles (30° or less), since the fix will vary widely under that circumstance with small errors in azimuth. The ability to visualize the situation from the plot is especially valuable in confined waters.

S.5 Planet Identification

While the Planet Notes in the opening pages of the *Nautical Almanac* usually enable you to identify the planet you are observing, it may sometimes be desirable, especially in conditions where only one quick sight is possible, to make an observation and confirm the identity of the body by computation afterward. In the case of the planets, it is normally sufficient to solve for just the declination in order to make a positive identification. This calculator program does that, using the DR latitude, the Sextant Altitude, and the approximate azimuth as entering arguments. The answer is then compared with the declinations shown in the planet listings in the Almanac's daily pages for the date and time of the sight. Figure 6-2 is an excerpt of the planet columns from the *Nautical Almanac* for May 31, 1979, in which this procedure can be followed.

MAY 31, 1979

G.M.T.	ARIES G.H.A.	VENUS −3.3 G.H.A.	Dec.	MARS +1.5 G.H.A.	Dec.	JUPITER −1.5 G.H.A.	Dec.	SATURN +1.0 G.H.A.	Dec.
d h	° ′	° ′	° ′	° ′	° ′	° ′	° ′	° ′	° ′
31 00	247 53.9	204 12.3	N15 09.9	209 05.8	N14 37.2	120 19.6	N19 39.1	88 00.5	N10 32.7
01	262 56.4	219 11.8	10.8	224 06.5	37.8	135 21.7	39.0	103 02.9	32.7
02	277 58.8	234 11.2	11.7	239 07.2	38.4	150 23.7	38.9	118 05.3	32.6
03	293 01.3	249 10.7 ··	12.6	254 07.8 ··	39.0	165 25.8 ··	38.8	133 07.7 ··	32.6
04	308 03.7	264 10.2	13.6	269 08.5	39.6	180 27.8	38.7	148 10.1	32.5
05	323 06.2	279 09.7	14.5	284 09.1	40.2	195 29.8	38.6	163 12.4	32.5
06	338 08.7	294 09.1 N15	15.4	299 09.8 N14	40.8	210 31.9 N19	38.5	178 14.8 N10	32.5
07	353 11.1	309 08.6	16.4	314 10.4	41.4	225 33.9	38.4	193 17.2	32.4
T 08	8 13.6	324 08.1	17.3	329 11.1	42.0	240 36.0	38.3	208 19.6	32.4
H 09	23 16.1	339 07.6 ··	18.2	344 11.7 ··	42.6	255 38.0 ··	38.2	223 21.9 ··	32.3
U 10	38 18.5	354 07.0	19.1	359 12.4	43.2	270 40.0	38.1	238 24.3	32.3
R 11	53 21.0	9 06.5	20.0	14 13.1	43.8	285 42.1	38.0	253 26.7	32.3
S 12	68 23.5	24 06.0 N15	21.0	29 13.7 N14	44.3	300 44.1 N19	37.9	268 29.1 N10	32.2

	S.H A. ° ′	Mer. Pass. h m
Venus	315 06.5	10 24
Mars	320 28.6	10 02
Jupiter	232 15.6	15 53
Saturn	200 04.6	18 01

Figure 6-2. Excerpts of daily pages from Nautical Almanac *listing planet declinations and SHAs.*

The calculator is "loaded" at the outset by entering the variable input data as follows:

DR Latitude (+/− if Lat. is S) ⎡2nd⎤ DMS·DD ⎡STO⎤ ⎡1⎤

Sextant Altitude (hs) ⎡2nd⎤ DMS·DD ⎡STO⎤ ⎡2⎤

Azimuth (Zn) (an estimate will suffice) ⎡STO⎤ ⎡3⎤

Then the program proceeds:

⎡RCL⎤ ⎡1⎤ ⎡sin⎤ ⎡×⎤ ⎡RCL⎤ ⎡2⎤ ⎡sin⎤ ⎡+⎤ ⎡RCL⎤

⎡1⎤ ⎡cos⎤ ⎡×⎤ ⎡RCL⎤ ⎡2⎤ ⎡cos⎤ ⎡×⎤ ⎡RCL⎤ ⎡3⎤

⎡cos⎤ ⎡=⎤ ⎡INV⎤ ⎡sin⎤ ⎡INV⎤ ⎡2nd⎤ DMS·DD

The answer displayed is the declination, with the proper sign, ready for comparison with the *Almanac* data, Figure 6-2.

Let's review a practical problem. On Greenwich date May 31, 1979, at a position near 41°N, 62°W, at 00ʰ GMT an observation of an unidentified planet is made with a sextant reading of 36°25.8′ at an approximate bearing of 265°. What planet is it? Running the data through the calculator program, the display indicates the body has a declination of 19°40′N, which compares, at 00ʰ GMT, only with *Jupiter,* thus identifying that planet.

Should the declination alone not provide positive identification, it is further possible, knowing the DR longitude and the GHA of Aries for the date and time of the observation, to find the approximate Sidereal Hour Angle (SHA) of the planet by using the same program as that for finding the SHA of a star, S.6. The figures for comparison, in this case, will be found in the box at the bottom of the *Almanac*'s daily pages, which lists the planets' sidereal hour angles and times of meridian passage. An excerpt of this table is also shown in Figure 6-2.

If, as is the more common routine, the navigator wishes to locate one or more of the navigational planets *before* making his observations, it is only necessary to enter the LHA, declination, and latitude at the approximate time of twilight (Program A.5) in the Sight Reduction Program, S.3. The resulting Hc and Zn will indicate the area in the sky in which the planet will be found.

This planet-identification program can also be used for the stars if only the declination is needed. It has the virtue of being short and simple. In most cases, however, you will require both declination and SHA for the positive identification of a star, and the next program, S.6, is designed for that purpose.

S.6 Star Identification

A common problem in making celestial observations of stars is the correct identification of the body observed. Before going on deck, and knowing what his approximate position will be at twilight, the navigator usually makes a list of the altitudes and azimuths of the stars he expects to shoot. These can be determined approximately by using a device such as a Rude Star Finder (described in *Bowditch*, Vol. I, 1977, Art. 2210) or, if using Vol. I of Pub. No. 249, by entering it with the estimated DR latitude and the LHA of Aries at the time of twilight, and extracting the Hc's and Zn's of the seven selected stars (see Figure 6-3). For a more complete explanation of these methods, the reader is referred to *The Yachtsman's Guide to Celestial Navigation* in this series.

LAT 41°N

LHA ♈	Hc Zn	Hc Zn	Hc Zn	Hc Zn	Hc Zn	Hc Zn	Hc Zn
	♦VEGA	Rasalhague	ARCTURUS	♦SPICA	REGULUS	♦POLLUX	Dubhe
195	28 08 062	24 23 094	63 04 138	37 39 173	42 29 245	25 51 286	62 43 330
196	28 48 062	25 08 095	63 33 140	37 44 174	41 48 246	25 08 286	62 20 329
197	29 28 063	25 53 096	64 02 142	37 49 175	41 06 247	24 24 287	61 56 329
198	30 09 063	26 38 097	64 29 144	37 52 176	40 24 248	23 41 287	61 32 328
199	30 49 063	27 23 097	64 56 146	37 55 177	39 42 249	22 58 288	61 08 327
200	31 30 064	28 08 098	65 21 148	37 56 179	39 00 250	22 15 289	60 44 327
201	32 10 064	28 53 099	65 44 150	37 57 180	38 17 251	21 32 289	60 19 327
202	32 51 065	29 37 099	66 06 152	37 56 181	37 35 251	20 49 290	59 54 326
203	33 32 065	30 22 100	66 27 154	37 55 182	36 52 252	20 07 290	59 28 326
204	34 13 066	31 07 101	66 46 156	37 52 184	36 08 253	19 24 291	59 03 325
205	34 55 066	31 51 102	67 03 159	37 49 185	35 25 254	18 42 291	58 37 325
206	35 36 067	32 35 102	67 19 161	37 44 186	34 41 255	18 00 292	58 11 325
207	36 18 067	33 19 103	67 33 163	37 39 187	33 58 255	17 18 292	57 44 324
208	37 00 067	34 03 104	67 45 166	37 33 189	33 14 256	16 36 293	57 18 324
209	37 41 068	34 47 105	67 55 168	37 26 190	32 30 257	15 55 294	56 51 324

Figure 6-3. Excerpt from Pub. No. 249 listing Hc and Zn for selected stars.

Stars can also be located ahead of time with your calculator, using the Sight Reduction Program, S.3, precomputing the approximate altitude and azimuth of any star just as though a celestial sight were being solved.

It happens, from time to time, that you shoot a star without the benefit of preidentification, and you need to determine exactly which star it is in order to complete the sight reduction. In this situation the reduction program is reversed, entering with the estimated latitude, the Sextant Altitude, and the approximate azimuth to obtain a declination and Sidereal Hour Angle (SHA), which can be compared with those given in the daily pages of the *Nautical Almanac* (see Figure 6-4).

JUNE 10, 1979		
STARS		
Name	S.H.A.	Dec.
	° ′	° ′
Acamar	315 38.3	S40 23.2
Achernar	335 46.4	S57 20.3
Acrux	173 37.9	S62 59.4
Adhara	255 33.1	S28 56.8
Aldebaran	291 19.4	N16 27.9
Alioth	166 43.2	N56 04.6
Alkaid	153 19.0	N49 25.2
Al Na'ir	28 16.0	S47 03.4
Alnilam	276 12.9	S 1 13.0
Alphard	218 21.6	S 8 34.3
Alphecca	126 32.5	N26 47.2
Alpheratz	358 10.3	N28 58.4
Altair	62 33.1	N 8 48.9
Ankaa	353 41.3	S42 24.9
Antares	112 57.6	S26 23.1
Arcturus	146 19.0	N19 17.5
Atria	108 22.0	S68 59.4
Avior	234 28.9	S59 26.9
Bellatrix	279 00.0	N 6 19.7
Betelgeuse	271 29.6	N 7 24.1

Figure 6-4. Excerpt from daily pages of Nautical Almanac, *June 10, 1979, listing Sidereal Hour Angles and declinations of all the navigational stars.*

Variations of most common sight-reduction formulae can be used for this exercise, solving first for the declination and, if that isn't sufficient—as it usually isn't—for the SHA to complete the identification. The formula for the first (declination) calculation is:

$$Sin^{-1}(\sin L \sin hs + \cos L \cos hs \cos Zn)$$

The program steps can be demonstrated by a practical example: In DR position 41°00′N, 70°30′W, an unidentified star is observed at Sextant Altitude 65°54′, bearing 151°. The time of the observation was 00ʰ56ᵐ34ˢ GMT, on June 10, 1979. The GHA of Aries on that date was 257°45.3′ at 00ʰ, and its hourly increase 15.041 degrees. Identify the star. The calculator sequence proceeds:

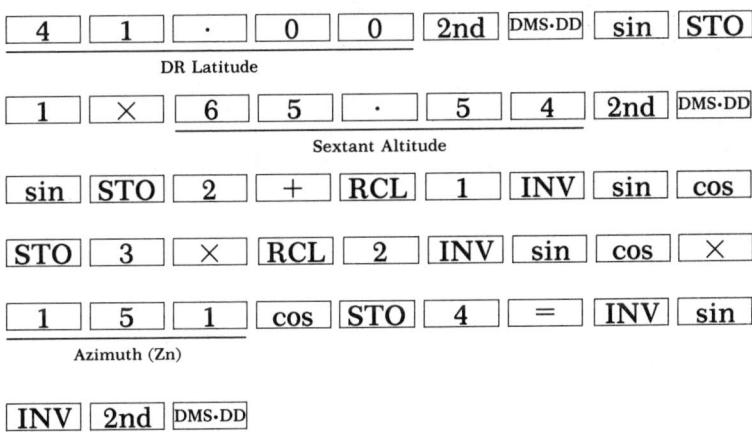

INV 2nd DMS·DD

The final display is the declination of the observed star, and, if the display after the ⌷ = ⌷ key was pressed was negative, the declination will be of *opposite* name to the latitude. In this example, the intermediate display was positive, so the final declination, 19°13.7′, is North, the *same* name as the latitude.

In this sequence you will notice the extensive use of the memory registers, even to the extent of recalling a natural function, inverting it, and then finding a second function —all to avoid having to enter the input data more than once. At the end of the first calculation, the contents of the four memory registers in use are:

Memory 1, sine of latitude
Memory 2, sine of sextant altitude
Memory 3, cosine of latitude
Memory 4, cosine of azimuth

By following this procedure, if the declination alone has not been sufficient for a positive identification of the star, the program can proceed to the second part, finding the Sidereal Hour Angle (SHA) of the star for comparison with the Almanac's listings. The formula for this second calculation is:

$$SHA = \tan^{-1}\left(\frac{\sin Zn}{\cos Zn \sin L - \tan hs \cos L}\right) + 360° - LHA \text{ Aries}$$

For our practical example, the keypunch sequence continues:

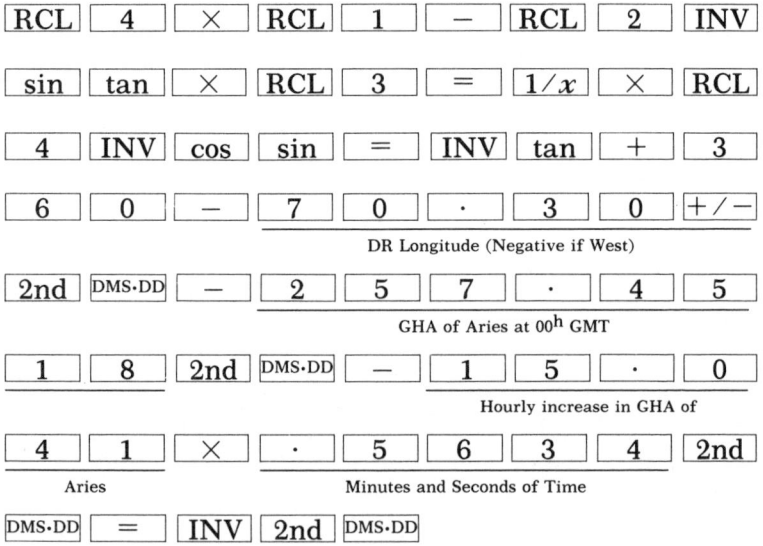

| RCL | 4 | × | RCL | 1 | − | RCL | 2 | INV |

| sin | tan | × | RCL | 3 | = | 1/x | × | RCL |

| 4 | INV | cos | sin | = | INV | tan | + | 3 |

| 6 | 0 | − | 7 | 0 | · | 3 | 0 | +/− |
DR Longitude (Negative if West)

| 2nd | DMS·DD | − | 2 | 5 | 7 | · | 4 | 5 |
GHA of Aries at 00ʰ GMT

| 1 | 8 | 2nd | DMS·DD | − | 1 | 5 | · | 0 |
Hourly increase in GHA of

| 4 | 1 | × | · | 5 | 6 | 3 | 4 | 2nd |
Aries   Minutes and Seconds of Time

| DMS·DD | = | INV | 2nd | DMS·DD |

The final display, 146°27.7′, represents the approximate SHA of the unidentified star. Referring to the *Almanac* star listing in Figure 6-4, it can be seen that, with a calculated SHA of 146°27′ and a declination of 19°14′N, the star must be *Arcturus.*

S.7 Sun's Azimuth

One method of determining the sun's true azimuth, a procedure practiced regularly at sea to check the accuracy of the compass, is by means of a sight-reduction calculation as explained in Program S.3. Another method, the traditional "time azimuth," obtains a direct solution and employs the formula:

$$Z = \tan^{-1}\left(\frac{\sin \text{LHA}}{\cos \text{L} \tan \text{d} - \sin \text{L} \cos \text{LHA}}\right)$$

The following rules must be observed with this formula:

- If the Local Hour Angle (LHA) is greater than 180°, subtract it from 360° and enter the remainder;
- If the declination (d) and latitude (L) are of *opposite* names, enter declination with a negative sign (as in Program S.3);
- If the computed azimuth angle (Z) is negative, add 180° *before* applying the rules to convert Z to Zn (shown below).

Looking at a practical example: What would the sun's true azimuth be at 17h18m07s GMT on May 17, 1979, at Latitude 41°00′N, Longitude 70°27′W? From the *Almanac* we determine that GHA (80°27′) minus longitude West (70°27′) equals LHA, which is 10°00′. By inspection, the declination is found to be 19°18.2′N. The calculator sequence is then:

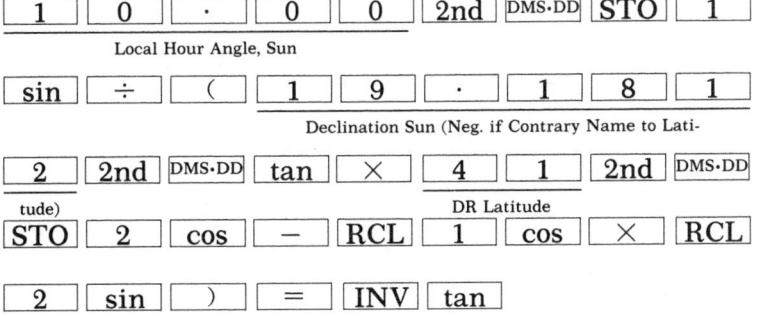

| 1 | 0 | · | 0 | 0 | 2nd | DMS·DD | STO | 1 |

Local Hour Angle, Sun

| sin | ÷ | (| 1 | 9 | · | 1 | 8 | 1 |

Declination Sun (Neg. if Contrary Name to Lati-

| 2 | 2nd | DMS·DD | tan | × | 4 | 1 | 2nd | DMS·DD |

tude)   DR Latitude

| STO | 2 | cos | − | RCL | 1 | cos | × | RCL |

| 2 | sin |) | = | INV | tan |

The answer displayed, −24.5, being negative, is corrected by adding 180° to obtain the azimuth angle (Z) of 155.5°. The following rules then apply to convert Z to Zn, the true azimuth:

$$\text{North latitude} \begin{cases} \text{LHA greater than } 180°, \text{Zn} = \text{Z} \\ \text{LHA less than } 180°, \text{Zn} = 360° - \text{Z} \end{cases}$$

$$\text{South latitude} \begin{cases} \text{LHA greater than } 180°, \text{Zn} = 180° - \text{Z} \\ \text{LHA less than } 180°, \text{Zn} = 180° + \text{Z} \end{cases}$$

Since, in our example, the latitude is North, and the LHA (at 10°) is less than 180°, Zn = 360°−155.5°, or 204.5°.

7. Practical Wrinkles

Until now our discussion has concentrated on the technical aspects of selecting and using a hand-held calculator for navigation, but we must not overlook the practical aspects of working with a calculator, particularly in the environment of a small boat.

First of all you should remember that your instrument is a fine electronic device and the environment of a small boat at sea is anything but ideal. It is important, therefore, to choose a place to operate where the calculator will be least subject to shock and moisture and where it will be suitably protected when not in use. One good idea is to make a holder that can be fastened to a convenient place on the chart table so that it will be handy to operate the calculator with one hand. Then, if you leave it for a moment, the instrument is not likely to fall to the deck. Some of the specialized navigational calculators are furnished with carrying cases, and these, affixed to a chart table, serve the purpose well. It goes without saying that protection from spray and spilled liquids is equally important in selecting your operating location, often easier said than found on a very small boat.

Despite the remarkable performance on a few low-capacity batteries, calculators do require energy, and usually the more sophisticated the instrument, the greater the power requirement. As a consequence, it is always a good idea to carry an extra set of batteries and a recharging device, too, if your manufacturer offers one for your boat's voltage. Some of the major suppliers offer 12 vdc chargers in addition to the standard 110 vac model, and these are particularly suited to small yachts.

I have found that a practical and efficient way to remember my programs is to list the steps in a convenient shorthand form on a left page of a pocket-size, loose-leaf notebook. Figure 7-1 shows a specimen page for Program S.5, Planet Identification. By leaving the right-hand page of the notebook blank, I can make notes as necessary of the variable input data, step through the program sequence following the notes on the left page, and record my answers in brief form with the input information. Since most hand-held calculators used aboard boats are not of the printing type, this is a useful way to keep track of a series of exercises, such as sight reductions, to which you might like to refer later. Some navigators prefer horizontal rows to vertical columns to lay out their programs, and some even reduce their memory aids to a single-column strip. The form is not important but the idea is useful if you need to recall the details of programs which you are not accustomed to working regularly.

Before undertaking a voyage during which you expect to rely in large part on your calculator for navigational information, it is wise to review your programs and, if they are new or if you are rusty, pretest them with some dry runs before you leave home. This way you will enjoy your full facility once you are under way.

In the course of your calculator exercises, you may well discover improvements in the approach or in the order of presentation of the sequences that will make the program shorter, more accurate, or easier to understand. You shouldn't hesitate to do this and even to attempt the creation of programs of your own because this is a great learn-

S.5 Planet Identification
(Algebraic Entry)

⟶ DR latitude, 2nd, DMS-DD, (+/- if S.), STO 1

⟶ Sextant altitude, 2nd, DMS-DD, STO 2

⟶ Azimuth, STO 3

RCL 1	RCL 2
Sin	COS
X	X
RCL 2	RCL 3
sin	COS
+	=
RCL 1	INV, sin
COS	INV, 2nd, DMS-DD
X	

Figure 7-1. Specimen notebook page for Algebraic Entry, Program S.5, Planet Identification (compare with Figure 7-2).

ing device and part of the fascination of working with calculators. But test any and every program thoroughly. Errors can occur and no machine can relieve you of the responsibility for the safe navigation of your vessel.

On the subject of programming, I am sure you will find as I have that an organized approach saves time and frustration. The usual steps in planning an original keystroke sequence are, first, to identify the information available and the terms in which you would like to express the answer. Next, the elements of the problem are stated in the form of a mathematical expression and the program of keystrokes worked out to solve it. Remember, there may be several ways to solve a given equation and you'll have an interesting time discovering the best one for you.

If your calculator has the capability of accepting a preestablished sequence in its program memory—the TI-55, for example, is keyboard programmable for up to thirty-two steps—you will also want to experiment with programming it yourself. Using S.5, Planet Identification, as an exercise, the TI-55 would be programmed with the following keystrokes:

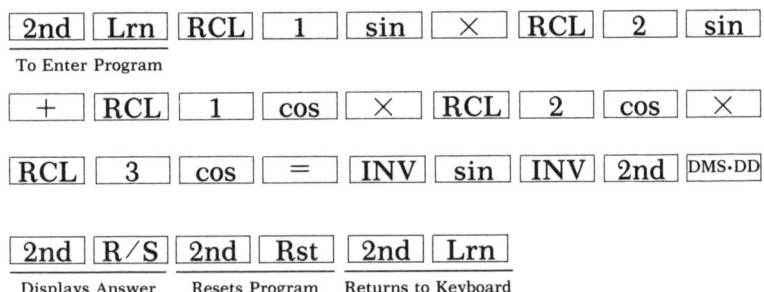

At the conclusion of the loading operation, press ⎡2nd⎤ ⎡Rst⎤ to reset to the start, enter the variable data into the appropriate memory registers, and press ⎡2nd⎤ ⎡R/S⎤, causing the program to be executed automatically. With the calculator on and programmed, try entering the data used in the S.5 practical problem and see if you don't get the same answer. The resetting step has been built into our

S.5 Planet Identification
(Reverse Polish Notation)

→ DR latitude f^{-1}, → D.MS, (CHS if S.), STO 1

→ Sextant altitude f^{-1} →DMS, STO 2

→ Azimuth° STO3

RCL 1	f, cos
f, sin	X
RCL 2	RCL 3
f, sin	f, cos
X	X
RCL 1	+
f, cos	f^{-1}, sin
RCL 2	f, → D, MS

Figure 7-2. Specimen notebook page for Reverse Polish Notation, Program S.5, Planet Identification (compare with Figure 7-1).

sequence, so each time you wish to run the program again you need only correct any variable data that has changed and press ⎡ 2nd ⎤⎡ R∕S ⎤—the calculator does the rest. While you will find that most navigation problems require more programming capacity than the TI-55 has because of the number of steps involved, the general principles apply to the more powerful instruments as well.

You may, in the process of developing programs, wish to work from the navigational formulae published in some detail in the classic texts, *Bowditch* and *Dutton,* or you may simply wish to restate existing programs, set up for operation with an algebraic entry machine, so they can be worked with the Reverse Polish Notation logic. The logics were discussed in Chapter 2 and, to offer a comparison for a complete program, the sequence from Program S.5, shown in notebook form for an algebraic entry calculator in Figure 7-1, is repeated in a form for an RPN instrument (this particular one for the Hewlett-Packard HP-65) in Figure 7-2. The mathematics are the same in each case—it is simply a question of the order of entry of data and the order in which the mathematical operations take place.

In either choice of logic it is also possible, and often useful, to "string" programs together—that is, to leave information from one program in the machine's memory registers so that the succeeding, allied program can be run without having to reenter repetitious data. This technique is used often in the programmable calculators when the steps in a large computation exceed the capacity of one unit "card." You will notice that our great-circle programs S.1 and S.2 are "linked" in this fashion.

Finally, no matter how much enthusiasm one expresses for the wonderful and extraordinary hand-held calculator, it must never be forgotten that calculators are electronic instruments and inevitably failures do occur—usually at the most inconvenient time. Every prudent navigator who goes to sea with a calculator carries the necessary tables or other equipment as a backup, and knows how to use them if the need should ever arise. Make sure your name appears among the prudent.